BOB BROWN

GENTLE
REVOLUTIONARY

BOB GENTLE
REVOLUTIONARY
BROWN

James Norman

ALLEN&UNWIN

First published in 2004

Allen & Unwin
83 Alexander Street
Crows Nest NSW 2065
Australia
Phone   (61 2) 8425 0100
Fax   (61 2) 9906 2218
Email: info@allenandunwin.com
Web: www.allenandunwin.com

National Library of Australia
Cataloguing-in-Publication entry:

Norman, James, 1970– .
Bob Brown: gentle revolutionary.

ISBN 1 74114 466 3.

1. Brown, Bob, 1944– . 2. Green Party (Australia). 3.
Politicians - Australia - Biography. 4. Legislators -
Australia - Biography. 5. Conservationists - Australia -
Biography. 6. Green movement - Australia. I. Title.

324.2940987092

Set in 12/15 pt Sabon by Midland Typesetters, Maryborough, Victoria
Printed by Griffin Press, Adelaide

10 9 8 7 6 5 4 3 2 1

Contents

The 'wellspring'

At a screening of forest films in Hobart in February 2003, around 50 people gathered to watch the documentary works by a local environmental film-maker. The films were screened in a large second-storey room above Paul Thomas's Rugs of Tibet shop down a small laneway off Harrington Street, central Hobart. Paul Thomas is Bob Brown's partner of eight years.

Understandably, after a week in Canberra in which he was called upon to answer for an anti-war movement, Bob didn't make an appearance at the screening until late in the evening. He made a short speech to the small crowd assembled there as one might speak with a group of close friends. And although the strains were showing after the week in Canberra, he offered some simple advice to those in attendance. 'Listen, if you feel just about ready to give up all hope, do what I do and spend a night out in the forest under the stars—it'll probably do the trick.' And therein lay the simplicity and steadfastness of Bob Brown—in one neat sound bite.

1

Over the past two decades, Bob Brown has been the stalwart who has carried the Greens banner all the way into the mainstream public spotlight; into the formidable position it now fills as the identifiably and unambiguously left-wing opposition party in Australian politics. This gently-spoken, bespectacled gay doctor from Tasmania has become something of a national hero of almost pop star status—respected even by those who diametrically oppose his politics.

It was frequently remarked throughout the 2000 federal election that two men stood out from the throng of federal politicians as noteworthy and successful in gaining the attention and respect of significant numbers of voters. They were John Howard and Bob Brown. By 2004, a revitalised ALP under Mark Latham had again reshaped the Australian political landscape. One of the first pledges Latham made on becoming ALP leader was to visit the Tasmanian forests with Bob Brown.

Howard is the long-surviving conservative Prime Minister, imbued with all the power and strength of a remarkable political strategist and survivor. Bob Brown's personal charisma is of an altogether different order. To his admirers he is seen as representing almost the antithesis of the brooding aggression or competitiveness that lies behind much of the 'political speak' commonly associated with politicians.

Brown is certainly not politically conservative, although in many respects he is very conventional. His conservatism is on the surface—conservatively dressed and mild-mannered, always clean-shaven, never publicly cussing. Yet the politics Bob Brown brings to the table are the politics of democratic revolution; the politics of sustainability over capitalism, of compassion over profit. His are the politics of optimism. Despite his mild-mannered veneer, Bob Brown will be remembered as one of Australia's true revolutionaries.

He frequently employs gentle humour, yet he is unwavering in his willingness to criticise those who only 'associate with the top end of town', as he frequently puts it. He is articulate in framing policy directions in the context of current, often local, voter interests, and consistently ties current issues back to his core concerns—Tasmanian forests and broader environmental issues.

His outspoken involvement in issues relating to the environment (and beyond) has led to his being recognised with a number of awards throughout his political life. These include being named Australian of the Year in 1983 by the *Australian* newspaper (and Australian of the Decade in 1990), winning the prestigious Goldman Environmental Prize in 1990, BBC *Wildlife Magazine*'s World's Most Inspiring Politician award in 1996, and being voted an 'Australian National Treasure' by the National Trust in 1998.

In 2002 Brown made the top ten list of 'Australia's Most Intriguing Gays' in *DNA Magazine*, and he was voted Australia's Most Culturally Influential Person by the *Australian Financial Review Magazine* in 2003. This grab bag of accolades indicates one thing—Bob Brown is both extremely popular and widely respected across a broad social spectrum.

There is more to Bob Brown's internationalism than merely holding a global perspective. He carries a global ambition for the Greens, as a force for a new kind of 'positive globalisation' in this century, a force with the potential to be every bit as significant as the labour movement was in the last.

But to his opponents, Bob Brown is a zealot, an extremist, and a serious threat. As the Greens have gathered increasing momentum as a political force, the more venomous the attacks on the party and its leader have become.

He has been bashed, threatened, and publicly vilified on numerous occasions. In November 2003 Queensland Liberal Senator George Brandis compared the ideology of the Australian Greens to the Nazis of 1920s and 1930s Europe, quoting verbatim from conservative *Herald Sun* columnist Andrew Bolt.

In response to such accusations of political manipulation and zealotry, Brown is unfazed. 'I'm not, [any of those things]

I'm a Presbyterian,' he told the *Australian* in 2000. He was referring to his conservative Presbyterian upbringing in rural New South Wales.

Bob Brown brings sincerity and dignity to political positions and a world view that many Australians would consider radical. He anticipates and disarms those who would wish to use the weapons of scandal or innuendo against him by, for example, announcing his homosexuality in his maiden speeches to both the Tasmanian and federal parliaments.

Brown's persona invites audiences, and the Australian public in general, to reconsider their own preconceptions about what is in fact radical. He creates the possibility of a different perspective; the formerly unthinkable can come to be seen as reasonable and rational. The shy, conventional side of Bob Brown makes it all the more surprising that he has emerged as such an outspoken activist.

Brown's own increasingly important role on the stage of Australian national politics has been associated with the rise of the Greens as a formidable force in Australian political life.

Perhaps the defining moment of this emergence of the Greens as an opposition party of substance in contemporary Australian politics occurred during the *Tampa* incident in 2001. At that time many ordinary Australians felt utterly appalled that the Howard Government had used images of boat people attempting to enter the country and made the claim that these refugees had deliberately thrown their children overboard in order to garner sympathy from the Australian public.

After some media-driven inquiry, it was widely accepted that the government had in fact overstated the children overboard claims for political leverage. The Coalition lost Peter Reith over the incident, but the Greens picked up new surges of voter support nationally.

It was this incident more than any other that gained the Greens the reputation of being the only party in Australian politics at that time willing to make unambiguous statements of condemnation of the Howard Government. The Greens echoed a national mood of appalled horror that the government would go to such lengths in its attempts to shore up support for its own controversial refugee policies.

Following this, Bob Brown was frequently called upon by the Australian media as the voice of credible dissent to the Howard Government, or 'the de facto Leader of the Opposition', as he has frequently been branded. This extended to a whole range of issues way beyond environmental politics—from detention centres, to foreign affairs matters, to the 'war on terror' and more broad-based opposition to the Howard Government's perceived lean to the right.

At the beginning of the twenty-first century, the 'war on terror' doctrine formulated by the US and embraced by the Howard Government means that new threats to world peace loom large. It is an era of unprecedented media-fuelled fear of global terror. The September 11 attacks on New York and the Pentagon ushered in a global climate of insecurity and threat, with massive knock-on effects. The doctrine of the 'pre-emptive strike' was the new and pernicious foreign policy coming out of the US during the Iraq War, effectively alienating and alarming the UN and much of Europe.

It is a period that has brought unprecedented turmoil, fear and anxiety globally. As far as national anti-war opposition is concerned, Bob Brown has been in the hot seat. In mid-February 2003 Brown addressed rallies right around Australia on Australia's involvement in the Iraq War. He always drew the loudest applause as he took his place on the podium, leading some commentators to observe, 'Bob Brown never meets a bad microphone'.

He spoke of this war not being Australia's war at all—but being the war of John Howard, Tony Blair and George Bush. He spoke of the need to allow the UN weapons inspectors to carry out their work in the Gulf. He spoke of the common humanity and people power of those marching 'for a better way'.

The Prime Minister has never, ever been given a mandate by the people of Australia to go to war with Iraq. He has no authority to turn his back on the wishes of the people of Australia. This Prime Minister has abused the terms of freedom and democracy in his own country. We are the human spirit around the world saying no to the impending holocaust. We want there to be a just community with the autonomy subjugated to it, not an unjust global economy with the people subjugated to it. So we say to Bush, and to Blair and to Howard—look at the European alternatives to war. Otherwise you will have the unnecessary blood of children in Baghdad on your hands, and the destruction of hope around the planet. No, of course we do not see you as a terrorist—but what do the mothers of Baghdad think? Have you asked them? Or have you not, like Saddam Hussein, have you not the heart to feel the terror of those mothers? I'd like to turn the Prime Minister's mind from the Bush White House, to the feeling of the people on the streets, where it is due.

In his distinctive way, Brown's words touched a nation, managed to cut through the cynicism many Australians feel toward politicians in general, and gave local voice and heart to a massive global movement that would come to be identified as the largest collective anti-war movement in history. The rallies he addressed in Melbourne and Sydney combined drew close to half a million people. Again, Brown was the revered spokesperson of the people on the streets.

Locally, both the ALP and the Howard Coalition Government have come to be seen as symptomatic of the drift toward centre right government politics taking hold globally, with a few notable exceptions such as Gerhard Schroeder's Social Democratic/Green coalition in Germany and Silvio Berlusconi's vision for a far right neo-liberal Italy.

Bob Brown symbolises for many the links between social justice, environmentalism in practice, and the glaringly urgent need for a vision of a better world. He is an almost isolated example of an activist who has made the monumental transition from local campaigner, to effective and visible national and even global environmental freedom fighter.

Certainly the Bob Brown we see—beamed into our lounge rooms as the environmental defender, lone voice in parliament speaking out for the rights of refugees or against Australian involvement in war—is only one side of the man.

It tells us nothing, for example, of the home-loving Bob Brown who enjoys thumping out a tune on his piano and speaks of having been 'set free out of a prison' on finding a loving relationship with his partner Paul Thomas. Or of the Bob Brown who prefers steak and three veg for dinner over tofu, any day.

Nor does it bring us closer to an understanding of this man who struggled with demons inside himself for half a lifetime, who considered taking his own life as a shy confused young doctor in Canberra, and who didn't enter a committed loving relationship until the age of 52. The same man who made the remarkable, quixotic transformation to where we find him today—in his political prime.

Indeed, the personal revolutions that have taken place inside Bob Brown have left him well-armed to foster more broad based, social revolutions in his public political life.

The one-dimensional media-constructed image of Bob Brown fails to discover the source from which he draws his inspiration and staying power to endure almost twenty years of parliamentary sessions and endless demands on his time from all manner of local and international organisations. That wellspring, one suspects, is to be found in those places in nature— from the Franklin River to the rocky razorback forest bluffs around his bush block in the Liffey Valley in central northern Tasmania—those sacred wild places to which Bob Brown has always been drawn, and to which he has dedicated much of his adult life to protecting.

There amid the rushing water and the awe-inspiring stillness of the natural world, a million miles from the sterile tedium of the nation's legislature, we come closer to understanding what truly drives Bob Brown.

Green Chapter 2
stirrings

As bushfires raged around the central west New South Wales town of Oberon two days after Christmas on 27 December 1944, Marjorie Brown gave birth to twins. First came Janice (Jan) then, half an hour later, Robert James Brown was born.

Jack Brown had moved his family—Marjorie and baby Ben—to Oberon just a year prior to the twins being born. Jack had previously worked for several years at Newtown Police Station in central Sydney. He would later tell stories to Bob about how members of the public too scared to make the journey home to the suburbs of Sydney had turned up in droves at the Newtown Police Station in 1942, when the city was shelled by the Japanese. Jack and Marjorie left Sydney in 1943, a time when Australia was deeply embroiled in war on two fronts, attracted by the relative calm and ordered life that awaited them on the New South Wales central tablelands.

The township of Oberon was a fairly typical small rural centre, complete with grand Victorian buildings dating back to the end of the nineteenth century, and a Roman Catholic convent, run by the Sisters of St Joseph, which is still in operation today.

Jack Brown, the junior of two local policemen and proud father, missed the twins' moments of birth as he was helping battle the fires, but fortunately their delivery was complication-free. Jack later complained at how 'bloody silly' he had been to be off fighting fires when he should have been back at the hospital, but such were the jack-of-all-trades demands placed on a man in his position. Jack later frequently joked that Bob proved early that he was to be 'always the gentleman', coming out half an hour after Janice.

On the day the twins were born, all over the state of New South Wales temperatures soared into the high thirties, as bushfires raged. In Sydney alone, the Fire Brigade reported receiving 74 calls to fires on 27 December, as blazes burnt out of control in North Ryde and Epping.

Yet despite the severity of the state's fires, all domestic news was pushed off the front page by reports of Allied assaults on Germany. 'Our planes made at least 4000 flights over the battle area and destroyed large quantities of enemy tanks and transport,' reported the *Sydney Morning Herald* on the day Bob Brown was born.

Bob Brown was born into austere rural lifestyle, fairly typical at that time. World War II was well under way in the Pacific and many Australian families were looking longingly to a time beyond the war, when they could steer their offspring toward the kind of life they themselves had known—social order with religious underpinnings and a unique kind of Australian conservatism with elements of a 'larrikin' spirit behind it. Many families had grown up with war as a part of life; memories of the Great War still figured largely in the psyche of Bob's parents' generation.

Jack Brown (himself the son of a policeman) was every bit the 'lovable larrikin'. He told Bob that on his way to the hospital after fighting the fires he was further delayed, getting caught up chasing a rabbit for a block toward the hospital.

When he was two years old Bob Brown's family moved from Oberon to Trunkey Creek, a small agricultural town on the old coaching highway between Bathurst and Goulburn, where his father received a new posting as the local policeman. It is from here that Bob's earliest childhood memories come into view.

Bob's persistent mental image from Trunkey Creek is of the bush that surrounded the small town. Much of it was etched in hues of ghostly grey and black from bushfires that had hit the area throughout the previous decade. But even as Bob and Janice were very young children, the burnt-out bushland was slowly rejuvenating itself with bursts of green—the new foliage of budding eucalyptus trees.

Trunkey Creek, with a grand population at that time of 121, was a former mining town, well past its boom days, home to a smattering of sawmillers and sheep farmers on small holdings. Some of Jack's police work involved dealing with drunks from Trunkey Creek's one pub—the Black Stump. As a youngster, Bob was shocked to witness his father putting down an out-of-control dog belonging to one of the drunks he brought back from the Black Stump. His father had wheeled the bloke back from the pub in a wheelbarrow.

Jack had an office at the front of an old brick police station. Bob has a strong mental image of his father, dressed in his police uniform, walking sheriff-like up and down the main street of Trunkey Creek. Although Jack Brown was undoubtedly an authority figure, he wasn't someone to be feared in Bob's childhood. 'Because of his authority . . . my father was someone who kept control but there was no great punishment [behind] that,' he says.

Jack would later tell his family stories of his youthful larrikinism—when he would jump on the back of the old Sydney trams for the sake of a 'free ride and bit of excitement'.

Bob was also to observe what he considered to be his father's fair treatment of criminals and suspects. On several occasions, Jack would come home to get a jacket to offer people he had arrested, so they could legally appear in court. Jack was a fair-minded policeman who would often let offenders off with a warning rather than pursuing matters to prosecution. 'As a little boy I wasn't as communicative as I could have been with him,' says Bob. 'But I did get a sense of a "fair go" from my dad.'

There was a safety and optimism in Bob's early childhood in the small rural setting of Trunkey Creek. Marjorie had come off the land, and so the family always had fresh butter, milk and eggs from the animals Jack kept on the property. By the time George was born in 1949, a tight-knit family unit had developed.

When Jack Brown took regular work trips to towns such as Bathurst or Sydney (which 'might as well have been Tokyo' as far as the Brown children were concerned) he would return with treats for the kids, Bob recalls. 'I can remember my father coming back from Bathurst . . . with . . . a bottle of lemonade, flavoured—it could have been lime or cherry cheer, whatever it was—for each of us when we were very tiny and, to keep this going, hammering a nail through the lid of the lemonade bottle so that you could suck through the lid and take it very, very slowly. It would go on for hours, dispensing of this little bottle of lemonade.'

From a very early age, although the twins were close, it became evident that Bob was more attached to his mother Marjorie, while Janice stuck closer to Jack. The pattern was to hold. Bob and Janice took to experiencing the bushlands close to the house together, although they quickly emerged as quite distinct character types. Bob says that while he was more of a dreamer, Janice was always more practical-minded—always busy doing things around the house, assisting on the domestic front.

The twins would take Sunday baths together, for which they would have to collect buckets of woodchips to heat the bath. Bob remembers that collecting the chips wasn't the twins' favourite job. On one occasion Janice screamed out after putting her hand directly onto the back of a frill-necked lizard that had made its home in the wood heap. On another occasion a giant rat had emerged from the feed bin. Bob, who reckons to have been four years old at the time, had the rat by the tail and wanted to bring it into the house. Janice insisted on having her own turn with the rat, but when Bob tried to give it over, the rat arched back up and bit her hand. The rat scurried away in fright, much to Bob's dismay—he had hoped to present the critter to his mother.

Bob's mother Marjorie was born on 27 April 1910 to Isabella and William Walton in Adaminaby, before they moved to Glen Innes. Her father died when she was just eleven. Marjorie was, controversially at the time she married Jack, a divorcee—her first son, Frazer Freeman, was Bob's eldest (half) brother. Jack Brown wasn't religious; it was Marjorie who had insisted that the kids went to Sunday School and church. The family had taken to attending the Presbyterian Church after the Church of England in Sydney refused to marry Jack and Marjorie because Marjorie was a divorcee.

Marjorie loved the bush and encouraged the kids, from a very early age, to think of nature as being at its best when left to its own devices. 'We didn't get very far if we picked snow-drops or other wild flowers and took them home because she'd very quickly tell us that they looked much nicer where they were, left alone. She'd say, "They are beautiful, but they are even more beautiful in the bush". She reminded me that they would only last a few days in a vase, but would last months if left alone. She certainly had a philosophy of liking the bush, and that made a big impression on me. It struck a logical chord that deeply impressed me,' recalls Brown.

One early event, perhaps Bob's earliest memory, saw Marjorie called to her young son's rescue as he was attacked by ants. 'This was before my third birthday. As I wandered . . . I came to [a] big open ants' nest, those big brown ants that are so common on the Great Divide, and wandered on to have a look, and then they were crawling all over me from head to toe and I just stood there with my mouth open and bellowed.'

Marjorie appeared through a gate into the paddock, picked Bob up in her arms, carried him into the house, stripped him off and dropped him into a tub of water to get all the ants off.

In that period at Trunkey Creek, Bob had his first exposure to the news of the time—old newsreels shown at the Bathurst picture theatre. At one screening, possibly of the Marx Brothers' *Duck Soup*, a newsreel of the Korean War had 'frightened him' with its depictions of 'these bombings and men in funny suits and guns going off and people obviously in really nasty circumstances'.

He also recalls the moving-picture men coming into Trunkey Creek and showing an early Australian movie with Aboriginal content—a 'fearsome portrayal' of Aboriginals burning settlers' huts, 'the whole misportrayal which is common to European so-called progress on all continents,' says Brown.

Jack Brown used to regularly read the comics from the *Sydney Morning Herald* to the kids, and Bob says he was 'galvanised' by listening to radio sports and news. Around this time, when Bob was about eight, his mother also told the kids about the death of King George VI and of Joseph Stalin, both of whom were fairly abstract figures in the juvenile minds of Bob and his siblings, although he says the death of King George was a matter of 'great sadness'. He had begun collecting pictures of the royal family from the front page of the *Women's Weekly*. These pictures and snippets of information he collected were 'just brilliant, brilliantly important things' to the young boy.

Bob started to get labelled around the house as something of an 'absent-minded professor', always twiddling his hair and increasingly withdrawn. Having previously been very closely connected to and dependent on his mother, Bob now started to enjoy his own company a lot more—taking walks alone around the Trunkey Creek property and venturing further afield. He was slowly becoming much more of a self-contained kid, with a wide-eyed curiosity for the wonders of the natural world, and a vague feeling of being something of a 'misfit'.

Although relations between all his family were always warm and supportive on the surface, Bob found himself spending more time alone. He felt an endless curiosity for the natural wonderland that surrounded him at Trunkey, coupled with a pronounced shyness toward anyone outside the family.

Although growing up in the bush, Bob was shocked by daily aspects of bush life. 'I didn't like guns and I didn't like the potential for violence. The gutting of rabbits I found a particularly putrid affair,' he says. 'I was much happier wandering in the bush, just wandering, looking at what was growing, what was moving around there, what could be done with it.'

He has a significant memory from 1952 that he says has always stuck with him, an early profound encounter with the restorative and inspiring aspects of the natural world.

'My parents must have been in Bathurst for some reason, and a robin redbreast's feather just floated down in front of me in the breeze. That I think just stands in my memory as clear as anything in my whole life; always has done. It's just the wonder of this thing floating down, floating down, and picking it up and feeling how soft was, holding it up and seeing it float down again, and the bright tuft of it . . . the bright red at one end and soft grey the rest of it.'

Perhaps even more remarkably still, he chose to leave the feather exactly where he had found it. 'Maybe it was the establishing of this relationship which was going on in my mind, that if I leave these things alone, they'll leave me alone but bring me inspiration and joy.' He had taken his mother's advice on board.

Although essentially conservative in manner and appearance, in their own distinct way Bob's parents both had a non-conformist streak. Marjorie had the still-recent history of being a divorcee, and Jack flouted convention by generating a second income despite being a policeman. He cultivated a chicken farm with several hundred birds which was 'against the rules for a policeman', according to Bob.

There were a few early indicators that the nervous, bumbling young Bob might also take a slightly different path to that expected of him. His father Jack never forced Bob to do things that he didn't wish to, like being involved in the killing and preparing of livestock. But animals were very much a part of life at Trunkey Creek. The kids knew to watch out for snakes and lizards and they lived with numerous farm animals.

At the age of six, Bob was put in jail for half an hour by Jack for not eating his spinach at dinnertime. 'It may have been half an hour, it may have been twenty minutes. I certainly came back and finished dinner off after it. I often laugh about that because it was . . . a great trial run for Risdon many years later.' Risdon was the prison in Tasmania where the Franklin protesters ended up spending time after getting arrested.

From this very early age, Bob and his siblings regularly attended religious services. He says his early concept of God was a very traditional one—the benevolent 'old man in the sky', responsible for all the good things, while the devil was waiting to pounce if you strayed, 'stoking the coals'. Up until his teenage years, when a more rational inquiring mind intervened, this belief in God was Bob Brown's 'bedrock'. He was taught all the Bible stories very early, said prayers every night, and by the age of ten or eleven couldn't understand how anybody could exist without believing in the Christian God. 'How could your brain stand the terror of a being in a godless existence?'

Perhaps this is partly why, rather than being a naughty child, Bob says he was always 'excruciatingly trying to be good'. Having a policeman for a father, he was always comfortable in the presence of police. This became evident later on a number of occasions when he was arrested in the course of his environmental and political activism. That ambivalent relationship with authority, and respect for the humanity behind it, is something that has only sharpened in later life.

❧ ❧ ❧

Bob can clearly remember the day he and Janice were given little box-like school cases and sent off to the Trunkey Creek Public School, about a kilometre down the road from their house. They became the newest additions to the total school population of 23 students.

For Bob, this was a matter of great anxiety. 'I was always very apprehensive about it. We were very shy kids, although Janice was a bit more rebellious than me. I would have preferred to have been left alone to get out in the bush or just read. I was terrified of all the new people I'd have to come in contact with at school.'

However, once he settled at the school, Bob was immediately singled out for his developing intellect, and even won an award for neatness in Grade 1. He developed a strange combination of competitiveness mixed with reticence and nervousness. Although he wanted to 'test things out to the full', he carried with him a distinct lack of confidence in his own abilities. This paradox of being a high achiever with a sharp intellect, yet crippled by an embarrassing shyness, was to plague him for many years to come.

Bob was already showing signs of being a good sportsman, and he can recall it was a 'matter of great importance' when he went off to Bathurst to compete for the Trunkey Creek School in a baton relay. He was a good runner, with his slender taut frame, and had been selected with Janice to run as one of the four Trunkey Creek representatives for the major competition. It still gives him a shiver today, he says, to recall how he managed to drop the baton on the last leg of the race.

'I learnt from that—even if you're way out in front, things can still go terribly wrong . . . All of a sudden the great public performance turned into a great public disaster. That upset me for about three months afterwards.' Bob was always more comfortable being a relay runner than performing as a solo athlete.

This love of athletics extended itself to a keen interest in national sports broadcasts on the radio. Bob clearly remembers listening to the Helsinki Olympics in 1952 with his ears glued to the family radio and feeling positively delighted when Marjorie Jackson won her two gold medals and Shirley Strickland won the 100-yard hurdle. He also shuddered with a knowing horror at hearing the Australian team drop the baton in the relay race.

At the age of seven in 1952, some of the certainties and securities that Bob Brown had enjoyed as a young child were about to be dashed. His carefree, idle days of wandering around the bush at Trunkey Creek were to become a thing of the past. The family, now made up of Ben (two years older than Bob), twin sister Janice, and younger brother George, moved to the bigger rural New South Wales centre of Armidale where Jack had been posted.

'Armidale was a shock,' recalls Bob, 'big town, no bush, moving into a haunted house'. The family moved into an old barracks building dating back to the 1860s and rumoured to be haunted. The conditions were much more cramped and less homely than their previous Trunkey Creek house. In addition, 'school became a terror'.

Early experiences at the school in Armidale jolted Bob Brown out of a blind faith in authority, as he was witness to kids being treated brutally by some teachers at the demonstration school for the Armidale Teachers' College. 'I got caned for . . . daydreaming and whistling through my teeth in the front row. Bang, down came the cane.' Despite his occasional daydreaming, Brown was a star pupil at the school, one of the top three students. But throughout that time, witnessing students being mistreated, Bob says he was visited for the first time with a new kind of ethical dilemma. 'It was very much fear-based disciplinary education,' he says. 'On the one hand I was wanting to do well, but on the other I was frightened of the teachers.'

One boy was caned daily by a particular teacher, despite the fact that he was suffering from hydrocephalus. Brown felt for the boy and wanted to take action. 'I was shy but I really wanted to go to the headmaster and say something about it but I wasn't game. So this was good store for later on because there's this tussle between: do you say something about it, shrug your shoulders [and say] it's somebody else's business, or is it your business? And it is your business.'

This might have been the first situation where Bob Brown was forced to place his own personal ethics above the accepted authority of the teacher. This was not an easy transition for a boy who had been taught not to question authority, and had hitherto been presented with no real reason to do so. His class was sometimes lined up and everybody would get caned because one student wouldn't own up to something. Bob says the school provided more 'stick' than 'carrot' education. He had to be sent home on several occasions suffering from stomach pains at merely witnessing the disciplinarian approach of the teaching.

These nerve-induced stomach complaints were to become more frequent as Bob Brown became increasingly ill at ease with his place in the world around him.

'When you're young time stands still, and it takes a hell of a lot of time to deal with things. Anxiety and chagrin about what went on there unfolded very slowly for me. At least I had the solid support and moral reference from my family. When I think of what it must have been like for those kids in the Stolen Generation, experiencing the same kind of Victorian [era] education, without the love of nearby family, I feel horrified.'

Despite speaking of having consistently close, cordial relations with all his siblings and parents, there was a rare brotherly tiff.

Bob recalls at the age of twelve having a fight with his big brother Ben, then fourteen, under the orange tree. Ben had been developing quite a skill in boxing from an early age, and he had set up a space in the garden bordered by a garden hose as a makeshift boxing ring. Ben directed Bob into the blue corner with a stool, while he stood opposite in the red corner. Ben had an alarm clock that would ring out to indicate the length of each round, and boxing gloves for each of them to wear. Bob was persuaded into the boxing ring against his better judgement, and before he was ready, Ben had struck him with a skillful left in the solar plexus. The two boys then began a more serious wrestle as Bob grew genuinely angry and forgot the rules. They were only broken up when Marjorie appeared on the side of the ring, beating both of them with the broom from the sidelines. It all came to an abrupt end when the three of them collapsed laughing. Nonetheless, Bob wasn't inclined to join Ben in his makeshift boxing ring after that.

School life at the Armidale Teachers' College demonstration school went from bad to worse for Bob. In that same year of 1956, he experienced sexual abuse at the hands of a male teacher who paid 'serial attention' to a number of boys at the school. 'When my turn came,' Brown says, 'it was not much more than him putting his hand up my trousers and handling my genitals and on one occasion vice versa in the dark at school'.

After the meetings with the teacher happened repeatedly over a period of weeks, the school headmaster arrived at the scene—a shed at the back of the school where the supplies were kept. 'The headmaster was obviously twigging to something. To me it was all inexplicable.'

A few days later, Bob was picked up by his father from an athletics meet in Sydney. He immediately knew something was up. His father and mother seemed deeply troubled as they drove home. A few days later he was pulled out of class and sent home by the headmaster, to find half a dozen officials including police gathered there in the lounge room. They entreated Bob to explain the nature of his relationship with the teacher.

Bob says that although he was a naive, innocent victim of the whole incident, he could see how troubling it all was to his mother and father. Jack began making arrangements to transfer his job, and thus move the whole family, to Bellingen, just south of Coffs Harbour. Apart from being told by his father that what had happened was against the law of God and man, there was little further discussion on the subject. 'It was a pretty terrible event for all involved,' he says.

Having been a top student throughout primary school, Brown says he was now seriously knocked off-kilter. In the first term at Armidale high school, Bob was the only kid in his year not making it through maths class. 'Although I can't measure it—I knew I was very distressed at the time—a really long-term psychological sequel of that event had set in as far as I was concerned, which was out of my control, quite beyond me,' says Brown.

After all the work his parents had done to shelter Bob from the darker sides of life, this single event was a watershed. 'I'd grown up with police and the notion of bad people and good people and here was a confusion, a crossover of events, and I didn't know where I stood on the spectrum,' he says.

In later years, he came to recognise that such events were part and parcel of the world he was growing up into, and that although there was no physical harm done, there were psycho-logical repercussions. He is quite clear about one thing, however—that his awareness of being homosexual was not related to this incident.

'That was a presumption . . . that my own sexuality was somehow triggered by that event. And it was quite clear to me that while that event occurred, the two things were quite separate,' he says. Brown says the impact of the event was very hard on his parents.

In retrospect, Bob says an eventual positive outcome of the event for him was that it 'knocked a bit of that competitiveness out of my career path and made me think on a much wider plane and brought me to ground as far as the way the world works'. He says he has wondered in later years if he may have ended up becoming a 'great surgeon and a conservative politician' had not those darker realities of life struck him squarely at that early age. 'That's where I was headed,' says Brown. Throughout his teenage years, from the influence of his parents, he was a political conservative, and a strong monarchist. 'You didn't discuss religion, politics or sex,' in that conservative world. But that single event simply 'knocked me flat'.

'I was brought up to believe that people who were in business, who were in politics, certainly in conservative politics, who were in positions of authority were right and that we supported them. I guess in some respects the incident with the teacher—although he wasn't a major public authority figure, he certainly was an authority figure in our lives as schoolkids—put one torpedo through the bow, at least of that ship,' he says.

Bob was 'struggling to contain' the inconsistencies of the messages he was getting from his church and his school about the world being a fair place, and the darker realities of life as he was experiencing it.

'It can't be overestimated what an impact that had on a pretty vulnerable, unworldly, sensitive young kid. But eventually . . . whether you resolve them or not, they are put behind you and you get on with life and career.'

A Chapter 3
troubled kid

By 1956, Jack and Marjorie Brown became increasingly concerned that they had a deeply troubled kid on their hands. Although they couldn't put their finger on precisely what it was that was troubling him, Bob was withdrawing further into himself, becoming increasingly distant from family and friends. Bob's parents were worried about him, and at a loss as to how to deal with their son.

Although Bob was never blamed for the incident with the teacher, it became a catalyst for the family to leave Armidale. By moving into the rural surrounds of Bellingen, Bob's parents were attempting to recreate some of the calm rural town life the family had previously known in Trunkey Creek.

Bob began at Coffs Harbour High School on the New South Wales mid-north coast halfway through first term in 1956. It was here, aged twelve, that he first met Judy Henderson, a young rural-raised girl who was to become one of Bob's closest lifelong friends. Henderson's first impression of Bob was of a very quiet, shy boy, who 'would always be looking out for anyone who was being disadvantaged in some way'. She knew nothing of the incident with the teacher at Armidale until many years later. It wasn't something he discussed with anyone until he was into his twenties.

Brown and Henderson both lived with their families in Bellingen, and would make the 30 kilometre north-eastern train journey together into Coffs Harbour every day. Bob's father Jack dropped Bob and his brother Ben off at the train station by car; Henderson would ride her bike. The train journey took over an hour each way, and this provided Bob with a welcome social outlet in which he could 'break out of himself' and forge connections with other kids out of the school context.

'I can actually remember the day he arrived at Coffs,' says Henderson. 'He was always slim, with a lovely smile, and very good-looking. At school he was actually very quiet, I can't remember him ever getting into trouble or anything like that. He was always very conservative and very shy, actually. He would always be looking out for anyone who might have been picked on and particularly make friends with that person. That was always what Bob was like, he always had this overriding concern for anyone who was silenced or in a minority.'

Henderson also got to know Bob's parents Jack and Marjorie quite well throughout this period. 'His father was always playing tricks on people,' she says. 'I remember he used to hide my bike, and I'd get back to the station at Bellingen from school and couldn't find it.' Henderson recalls another occasion where Jack had picked up Bob and his brother from the train, and she had headed off in the other direction on her bike. The next minute she saw them come racing back down the road 'with the kids hanging out the window', hot on the heels of a stolen car. Jack had picked the numberplate as belonging to a stolen vehicle, and it didn't matter that the kids were in the car—he was in hot pursuit.

'The whole family have a wonderful sense of humour,' says Henderson. 'Marjorie was just an extraordinary woman; very calm, but with a delightful sense of humour.'

She remembers one night when a kerfuffle broke out between Jack and a drunk in the street in front of the Browns' house. 'Marjorie looked out the window to see Jack on the ground with this fellow on top of him thumping him in the head,' she recalls. 'Marj walked over with the handcuffs and casually slipped them on this guy who was pummelling her husband. That was the sort of person she was.'

By the middle years of high school, Bob had begun to re-establish his confidence and found himself, along with Judy Henderson, consistently among the top two or three students academically at Coffs Harbour High School. He also flourished in the school athletics team, particularly excelling in sprint racing and hurdling. Bob was forever jumping over homemade hurdles at the house in Bellingen.

Although he says his home life was excellent at Bellingen, he was still 'brewing a lot in his chest' from the turmoil that had taken hold inside him. 'I was very lucky that I had such accommodating parents. They had moved from Armidale to Bellingen because of the turmoil I was in. From their perspective, they had a youngster who was achieving well, but for some reason or other was a misfit,' he says.

Marjorie and Jack would frequently take Bob aside and ask him: 'Is something the matter?' 'What is troubling you?' 'The easy answer was always no, I'm okay,' says Bob. 'But of course I wasn't okay.'

Bob reckons he became aware of his homosexual orientation from the age of twelve, yet he had no recourse whatsoever to discuss the matter with anyone. He had secretly found a book on sex education at a relative's house, and had read that anyone with a homosexual inclination should seek professional medical help and treatment. 'Increasingly,' says Bob, 'I was a very disturbed kid. I was extremely clear that the world just didn't add up—everyone is not equal, everyone is not treated equally. And that some of those differences could get you into real trouble.'

The only place people even talked about sex at that time, says Bob, was in the schoolyard, where any mention of homo-sexuality was delivered as a jibe. 'But at least it was mentioned,' says Bob, 'even the jokes were better than complete silence.' There was some intimate contact with other boys at high school, although nothing more than teenage contact. 'I was waiting for something to turn up and give me clarity, but of course it didn't.'

Despite his inner anxiety and the feeling of being locked into a cell as a young gay person in the 1950s, it was not a period of abject wretchedness. There were many aspects of life that Brown thoroughly enjoyed as a teenager—sports, academia and current affairs. He took to reading widely—newspapers, magazines, encyclopedias. 'I was interested in the lot. I devel-oped a very wide knowledge of history,' he says.

Brown and his friend Judy Henderson both joined a church youth group called the Presbyterian Fellowship, but Hender-son says it was ostensibly just a young people's social club. 'Bob wasn't a religious fanatic as a teenager, and he certainly became less religious as the years went on,' she says. 'In fact I remember him saying to me, if there was a god and he ever met him, he'd kick him in the shins.'

Both Brown and Henderson came from Liberal/Country Party voting family backgrounds, with Robert Menzies an 'incredibly imposing figure in our lives'. They would both listen to Menzies on the radio during parliamentary question time, and Bob listed the conservative prime minister as one of his key early influences.

But Henderson says that Bob's brand of conservatism and religious underpinning found expression through more secular means. 'Fundamentally, he was very conservative. He still is small 'c' conservative—conservative dress, conservative hair-cut, always clean-shaven, and shy. But what would stir him into action was when he saw the voiceless in society, in the street or in the classroom, being picked on. That's the trend that has continued through to this day.'

Henderson recalls Bob telling her that he wanted to find a cure for cancer when he grew up. 'He disputes that he ever said that,' she says. 'But that, to me, was just an early indicator that he really wanted to do something that was important, to do something for the rest of society.'

At the age of fourteen in Year 9, Brown won an academic prize for diligence in reading and writing. He was awarded a book voucher. On the next summer holiday trip to Sydney with his family Bob went into a bookshop and exchanged the voucher for *Tales of Horror and the Supernatural*, a compilation of short stories by writers such as Edgar Allan Poe and H.P. Lovecraft.

The librarian at Coffs Harbour High told Bob he ordinarily wouldn't have allowed him to get that book, but seeing as he'd already bought it, he was allowed to read it. Feeling something like a misfit himself, the Gothic literature struck a chord with Brown, who had already read stories by the Brothers Grimm and Aesop's Fables. Brown says he found this literature contained more salient lessons about life than the religious instruction he'd been getting.

Bob became the junior prefect at Coffs Harbour in Year 11, an honorary role generally given to kids before becoming school captain in their final year. Whilst in that final year at Coffs, Bob remembers, a female history teacher came to the school wearing a communist badge on her lapel. Bob vividly recalls the sensation of it among other staff and some students; the outraged whispers in the hallway. The history teacher turned out to be one of the best teachers he'd ever had, one of 'those special teachers who actually speak to students like they are equal people'.

Brown says he was well familiar with what communism had done overseas, and the stigma attached to the label 'communist' in that early Cold War period was extraordinary. Although taken aback by learning history from someone with communist sympathies, he immediately listened to her with an especially keen interest, and ultimately respected her opinions more than those of any other teacher in the school.

Jack Brown received another transfer, this time to Windsor on the outskirts of Sydney, meaning Bob and his siblings would transfer to Blacktown High School. Remarkably, even though he was only a student there for his final year, Bob was made school captain at Blacktown in 1961. In that same year he also won the intermediate 120-yard hurdle race at Penrith Regional Athletics Carnival.

Bob wouldn't have minded being made school captain at Blacktown, except that he was aware of the unfairness of the appointment. He became great friends with another boy named Kevin Stephenson. An election had taken place in which Stephenson was voted captain by the students, but the teachers and principal of the school had overruled it. Bob had come from Coffs Harbour with a glowing recommendation and high academic results, whereas Stephenson was considered more of a troublemaker. Brown was the safer bet from the school's perspective.

It was to Bob's way of thinking an unfair and corrupt abuse of power, a major travesty of the democratic process. The nature of his appointment to captain placed him in a deeply compromising position, adding to his already awkward sense of himself within the new social environment.

Incensed by the decision, Brown waited outside the principal's office to protest, but the principal refused to discuss it. He says it took a courage of which he was barely capable, on a par with standing up to George W. Bush many decades later, to raise a voice of protest with that headmaster in Blacktown.

Finally Brown did get to see the principal and was told, 'You're captain and that's all there is to it'. He felt angry and ashamed about how things had turned out. It was just another example in the young Bob Brown's mind of the abuse of authority. When it came to delivering his acceptance speech, an attack of nerves and a flaring of his stomach pains rendered him incapable of delivering the speech.

Apart from involving himself in sports, Bob put his head down that year and achieved high academic grades. Inside he was feeling torn apart.

But it wasn't the last that the school staff would hear of the injustice of the school captain election. It led to an end-of-year rebellion by the final-year students, which Bob was very much part of. The students wired up the school's speaker facilities for the final assembly in the courtyard. Just as the headmaster was about to address the assembly, out through the loudspeaker bellowed the Sorbent toilet tissue advertisement. '... *What's the gentlest tissue, From the bathroom you can issue? Why it's Sorbent, Sorbent for sure ...*' Meantime the girls had put purple dye throughout the school's water system.

All the students at the assembly, including Bob who was on stage beside the staff, broke into hysterical laughter. There was deep horror among the school's administration. The principal immediately threatened that leaving certificates would be denied all the students, and none of them would be given references from the school. Bob says it was a significant event in the history of Blacktown High, at that time the biggest high school in New South Wales.

❧ ❧ ❧

Despite the threats from the Blacktown High principal, Bob Brown won a Commonwealth scholarship to study medicine at Sydney University—as did his old Bellingen friend Judy Henderson—in 1962. He had in the back of his mind that perhaps he might be able to do some missionary work down the track with a medicine degree, and be of some practical benefit to society. But he applied for medicine mainly because he had no idea what else to do with his life, and his mother and the local pastor advised him it would be the best thing to do. He was in the throes of deep-seated inner turmoil.

Undertaking his medical degree at the age of eighteen, it was the first time Bob was to live away from home. He found an elderly couple in Sydney to board with. It was the first of a series of flats he would board in over the next four years. It was a deeply unsettling period, in which he moved from one boarding situation to another—an elderly lady in Bondi, another old lady in Marrickville, then a couple living out past Rockdale. Although most of the landlords had looked for boarders to give themselves extra company as well as income, there was no-one Bob could really relate to, no other young people he could talk to about his personal problems.

Bob says his developing sexuality was becoming an increasingly debilitating and isolating burden to bear. He hadn't discovered anything like gay bars or clubs in Sydney—about the closest he got to sexual intimacy was anonymous men putting their hand on his lap in theatres—and he says he'd immediately flee from the cinema in fear.

Out of desperation he wrote a long anonymous letter to the *Daily Mirror* in response to a particularly nasty homophobic editorial the paper had published. In the letter he wrote about what it was like being in that circumstance, and a lament about God having made him that way. He articulated a plea that a more civil, accommodating attitude was required from society rather than the hateful attitude the paper had expressed. 'It was the sort of thing that now seems quaint, but it was the best point of reference I could give it at the time.' His letter went unpublished.

Judy Henderson recalls that the period spent studying medicine in Sydney was 'a terrible time' for both Bob and herself. Bob says it was 'about the worst period of my life'.

'We both had to win scholarships to get to university, so financially it was very hard—we never had any money,' says Henderson. 'Socially it was abysmal. We were both from the country, and had terrible difficulty adjusting. For Bob, the growing recognition of his sexuality was very difficult within the family setting; his father in particular would not have been accepting of that . . . People talk about having a wonderful time at university, but it was just really awful for both of us—so competitive and socially awkward.'

The beginnings of 1960s liberalism had started to kick in. Brown did read with interest some of the radical ideas being presented in the university newspaper, *Honi Soit*, and paid some attention to debates and discussions taking place on the university campus. These discussions included creationist versus humanist discourses—ideas that swirled around Bob's head, striking chords in his inquiring mind. It was a period of social permissiveness, says Bob, but he still had the bigger problem of his sexuality to deal with. Even in the progressive university climate, there seemed to be no help on hand for young homosexuals. The sexual revolution had made inroads in Australia, making way for a gay rights revolution that would take hold throughout the following decades. 'Talking about sex in all its manifestations was becoming much more acceptable,' says Bob.

However, his shyness and questioning of his religious faith rendered him pretty detached from university social life. Bob says he did have good friends at university, and he wonders now if he would have even survived without them. 'Although I didn't talk to them about my homosexuality, they must have wondered at times, especially at certain social events. But I really don't think I'd be around now if they weren't there for me back then.'

Bob joined the university athletics club for a short spell. At one of the first meetings for the year of 1963, everyone in the club had to stand up and say what they were good at. 'These quite self-confident guys had got up thumping their chests about what they were going to do,' says Brown.

'And I got up and said, "Well, I'm going to have a go at the 100 metres and if I'm no good at that, I'll try the 400 metres. If I'm no good at that, I'll have a go at the discus and if I'm no good . . ." I went through the whole range and obviously wasn't much good at anything but was prepared to have a go at the lot.'

Quite innocently and earnestly, Bob Brown had managed to get the whole room in a hysterical state of laughter. However, he says that owing to his inner confusion—'I was so out of it by this stage'—he didn't perform well at athletics meets and ended up leaving the club soon after. Bob was slowly but surely withdrawing further into himself—he still struggled with religious questions, felt utterly isolated in his home life, overwhelmed by the demands of the medical studies, and distraught and isolated over the question of his homosexuality.

At this stage of his life he 'wasn't sure of anything'. He was still in conflict with deeply ingrained Victorian ethics, as he says many people were in Australia in the early 1960s. Although he had decided he had to part ways with the church, he still felt the pressure of it in his life—that 'behind it all was some sort of damnation. There was no answer to those questions, and in fact, with a mature look at it, I can see now that religion was very much part of the problem.'

'As I got towards twenty . . . what became increasingly apparent was the inability to settle the two bulwarks of the concept of God . . . one is that God is good and the other is that God is almighty . . . [but] if you're almighty you're responsible for the lot. And if you're responsible for the lot, you're not good,' says Brown.

These universal questions about the nature of God went round and round in Bob Brown's head for many years. How could God allow such monstrous evil and destruction to go on in the world? How are we to trust people in authority or within the church when experience has taught us otherwise? Why would a benevolent God allow human injustice and suffering to run rampant?

Eventually he summoned the courage to put to a young religious teacher in Bondi a question that left him certain he could no longer accept the church's dogmas. He asked her about the Polynesians that Captain Cook had encountered on his Pacific voyage. They had never heard the name of Christ; did that mean they were destined to go to Hell? He remembers her answer vividly: 'They went to Hell because the Bible says you can't get to heaven except through knowing the name of Christ'.

Perhaps it was the evidence Bob Brown was looking for to confirm that he could no longer believe. He realised that the comfort from the church only came as a result of 'putting a clamp on your own intellect and your own reason'. Brown says he was also aware that 'there is no uniqueness in anyone's circumstances on this planet'.

Therefore, he no longer wished to be part of a church that would condemn people irrespective of their life circumstances. Moreover, his own life circumstance in regard to his sexuality was looming large as something for which he would stand condemned by his own church.

'I didn't want to be part of a belief system that required you to mould your life according to it but didn't deliver as it said it would when you were in trouble yourself,' he says. The Bondi incident was the breaking point. For the shy, troubled young Bob Brown, it had taken Herculean courage to even put the question to the young religious teacher.

❧ ❧ ❧

Bob has vivid memories of just wandering around the streets of Sydney feeling utterly overwhelmed by the wretchedness of his situation. The questions of religion and sexuality seemed beyond resolution. There was no-one he could turn to for help. Finally, says Bob, 'the patent absurdity of dogmatic religion finally began to dawn on me'.

Bob continued carrying around the 'private burden' of his undisclosed sexuality, while simultaneously finding peace and solace in trips up to the bush—specifically to his aunt and uncle Bill and Lily Walton's property in Glen Innes. He says the regular trips he would take to Glen Innes were an enormously important source of rejuvenation at this stage of his life. 'It was the most wonderful place on earth for me. That was spectacularly important . . . there were kangaroos up there, there were snakes, wallabies, echidnas, the whole works, and nobody, nothing else. You'd strip off and go for a swim in one of the creeks . . . and I was let do what I wanted to do,' he says. The strength that Brown finds in the restorative power of nature has since become a constant theme throughout much of his professional life.

Although he made a few good friends throughout the years at medical school, 'this constant of the bush and its changing seasons was something special beyond all things . . . a place of refuge in a way . . . and a place of continuity . . . which was a great giver of strength. It gave . . . a reason for existing, to continue to exist when at times I got to the point of wondering what was the point of it, [I'd] grown up full of expectations in life and then finding them for one reason or another dashed or blighted in a very critical period.'

Beyond his own internal turmoil, Bob had started to feel more deeply affected by global events. He says he remembers sitting with a friend and hearing about the Cuban missile crisis, and wondering how long it would be before 'they started dropping bombs'. Newsreels had also started coming through showing scenes of the poverty of Palestinian refugees. 'I didn't understand what it was all about, but I did understand that there were people in the world living in disgusting circumstances beyond their control and we should do something about it if we could. I thank the church for that,' he says.

It is significant that even as a teenager, but more so in his twenties, Bob Brown developed a profoundly rationalist approach to religion and world affairs. He began asking deeply philosophical questions about the meaning of life, but his approach to those questions was to become increasingly secular. Moreover, while the church had let him down on a number of fronts and his own reason had drawn him away from the church's dogmas, his affinity with nature was something that stayed with him from his childhood into his early adult life.

Even at university, Brown was getting lessons in the 'unfairness of the world', and the importance of circumstance and contacts, over real virtue. Fearing a flooding of the medical profession, Sydney University failed over 50 per cent of its students in the first two years that Brown was there. He was shocked at the patent unfairness of the 'lotto-like' procedure. After failing a few subjects in his first year, (including scoring 32 per cent for Chemistry in his first semester) Brown learnt that the only way to pass was to lock himself in his room for weeks before the examinations and simply learn all the facts by rote.

'There I was at medical school because it was the right thing to do, not because I had any great proclivity for it,' he says. He was also given an early lesson in the workings of the world at medical school when one of the tutors gave some students attending special classes a copy of one of the exam papers prior to sitting the exam. 'It wasn't that the [other students] were worse . . . but they were getting knocked out because . . . they didn't have the right contacts,' he says.

Having parted ways with conventional religion, Bob nevertheless clung to his conservative politics into his twenties. He voted for the Country Party, and even tried to join the Liberal Party on a number of occasions unsuccessfully, purely owing to circumstance. The events of his unsuccessful attempts to join the Liberal Party seem uncanny, bordering on the absurd. Firstly, in Sydney, Brown simply couldn't find the Liberals' office. 'I went down to Ash Street or Bridge Street in Sydney and couldn't find the place,' he says. The next attempt came a few months later in Canberra, when Bob was working at the Canberra Hospital. This time he found the party office, but arrived there two or three minutes past five and was told: 'I'm sorry, we're closed. Could you please come back again?' He never did make it back.

Brown says around this same time he was invited to several conservative functions such as those organised by the Australia/America Society, but felt increasingly uncomfortable there. 'At least I was beginning to recognise that wasn't where I should be,' he says. He was deeply torn between his career path as a young doctor nearing the end of his studies, and the tussle of an increasingly uneasy, inquiring mind left wayward and anchorless following the departure from religious certainty.

By 1968, having miraculously scraped through at the University of Sydney, Brown became a young registrar at the Canberra Hospital. He had applied for posts at Prince Alfred and Sydney hospitals; Canberra was his third choice, but in retrospect he considers it to have been a very fortunate outcome. He moved into the residents' quarters—then part of the hospital—that sat alongside Lake Burley Griffin. The graduates worked in excess of 100 hours a week.

Still lacking in confidence and suffering intense shyness and social ineptitude, Brown at least found some respite in having bought a car and being able to get away to visit his parents and family, who were then living at Dundas. He made frequent trips away, solo or with hospital friends, to the Brindabellas and Tinderys National Parks.

At this time the Vietnam War was well under way, and one of Brown's duties was to conduct draftees' physical examinations. He'd only missed out on the draft himself by four days.

He says the Vietnam War and the demonstrations that took place around the country—particularly one he attended in Sydney when US President Lyndon Baines Johnson ('LBJ') came to Australia and there were estimated to be one million protesters—helped to galvanise his politics away from the conservative side. Bob's father Jack was now a policeman in Sydney, and he told Bob how he hated having to arrest conscientious objectors. Jack experienced the first of a series of heart attacks through this period. Bob suspects his ethical dilemma at how to deal with the conscientious objectors was part of the reason behind Jack's failing health.

Although his politics were still largely undeveloped, Brown did take the liberty of bending the rules and citing conditions such as 'acne' as medical grounds for recommending against compulsory conscription. His time of reckoning had arrived. 'I was faced with real live people who were being sent off to shoot other people or be shot themselves. Some of them wanted to go and some of them didn't.'

Brown used his position of authority within the hospital to do what he felt was morally appropriate. 'At least there was an arrangement that made sense: pass those who want to go, no matter how flat their feet are or how poor their physical condition might be, and fail those, no matter how healthy they are, who particularly desperately didn't want to go.'

Brown says he was 'torn' by seeing Bob Menzies on television pushing the line that Australia must go to war to protect its sovereignty, and yet also seeing on the screen the horrific Vietnam War images that were beginning to trickle in. He eventually arrived at his own position that 'this [was] a cruel, unwarranted, destructive, awful, unchristian war that we're involved in'.

While at Canberra Hospital, Bob's repression and angst over his sexuality reached a head—and he ended up in hospital with fulminant colitis—a condition he puts down to stress and anxiety.

The notion of suicide had floated through his mind on numerous occasions throughout his years at Sydney University, but the temptation became stronger in Canberra. Eventually, he found himself standing beside Lake Burley Griffin pondering how far he would have to swim out before he would reach the point of no return.

'It was totally related to the stress of that social isolation that I found myself in . . . it is impossible to tell somebody who didn't exist then what it was like as far as my experience of it and the experience of many of my contemporaries . . . many of them remember this same ordered society, a society which was very readily able to galvanise itself and go to war, where it had an identity related to Britain and the empire . . . and yet was repressing itself from all sides,' he says.

'I was very lonely in terms of not being able to talk about sexuality, but I wasn't lonely in the sense that I always had good friends who I enjoyed spending time with. They didn't ask questions, and that was part of it. They knew something was going on. I'm convinced I wouldn't have survived without them.'

Bob was simply unable to make the leap to talk to anyone about his sexuality. He says the world in which he had grown up as a homosexual is as hard to imagine as it is to imagine the world without cars today. 'Even just to think back on it causes me some upset now. Think of Iran today with people getting hung, then you can start to imagine Australia in the 1950s and 60s for gays.'

Bob couldn't see it then, but help was on its way. Only he would have to travel thousands of kilometres away to the other side of the world in order to find it.

London Chapter 4
to Liffey

T he spirit of revolution and psychedelia was potent in the air in 1970 in England when Bob Brown arrived fresh from Australia as a young doctor, aged 25. It was the breathing space he so desperately needed after the sterile claustrophobic world at Canberra Hospital, and the social isolation and repression he had felt at the University of Sydney.

Bob says it would have been a great time to be in London for people looking for an exciting social life immersed in the spirit of the 'swinging sixties', but in his case it was more a matter of searching for escape.

Although the world Brown landed in was far removed from the 1960s free-wheeling idealism that fellow Australian expats such as Richard Neville and Germaine Greer personified, London at least gave Brown the distance he needed to start to sort himself out.

In coming to London, Brown says he was attempting to 'break out' of his social conditioning: 'This feeling that you owe it to society, yourself, your family and everybody else, to go on and be a specialist and to follow the logical progression through the medical sphere . . . till you end up with a plate up and the Jaguar—British racing green—car on the North Shore.'

The first obstacle he encountered in England was the revelation that his work papers were not valid. The medical administration in London wouldn't accept his photocopied medical identification papers so Bob had to write to his mother back home to get the originals posted over from Australia. In the meantime, he had to take a job at the Cornhill Insurance Company 'licking stamps and putting them on envelopes' for £11 a week. The job, menial as it was, lasted several months. Despite it being a very formal office, Bob recalls that he would walk in each morning and say 'G'day' to the office staff. He was roundly ignored, except for a West Indian chap who would laugh and say 'G'day' back.

Initially, he went to see a series of psychologists in London, still seeking help on the issue of his homosexual inclination. One of the doctors tried to encourage him to think more positively about his sexuality. The psychologist suggested that Bob try to enjoy who he was, rather than fighting his nature. It was the advice he needed to hear. Brown recalls the London psychologist telling him: 'Look Bob, instead of fighting it, why don't you make a good thing out of it. It's part of who you are. Accept yourself. Not only that, enjoy it!'.

'Shocking as this sounded,' Brown recalls, 'it knocked down another barrier. I met some other homosexuals and began to see the light. Progress, however, was slow.'

He was nowhere near ready to have a relationship. 'Those experiences were for better or for worse, like everybody else. I wasn't into forming a relationship then, and not for a long, long time after . . . in what still felt to me like a pretty hostile world.'

However, Bob finally did carve for himself something of a social life. He met other expats who were having exactly the same experience. They had come to London from places as far afield as Spain and Canada to try to resolve their sexuality issues in a progressive, cosmopolitan environment. 'I think through meeting other gay guys, I got a certain confidence back. I was starting to talk to people overtly about the fact that I was homosexual.'

It was also the first time Bob smoked pot, with a group of Somali students. He did inhale, but it didn't really do anything for him, so he was rarely drawn back to pot smoking after that. 'I noticed all the counter-culture around me, but I wasn't really a part of it,' he says. When he did summon the courage to attend social functions or underground events he 'felt like a fish out of water'.

It was a whole new world that Bob Brown had landed in, and he was wide-eyed with the wonder of it all. He was very alert to the changing times, and the political paradigm shifts occurring around him. He had started buying progressive magazines including *Oz* and the Australian magazine *One Nation*, magazines that both gave him a connection with home and presented political positions he was increasingly relating to. 'These magazines were at the forefront of political satire, and I was fascinated by them,' says Bob.

After his official medical papers arrived from Australia, he took a number of posts, including at St Mary Abbott's Hospital in Kensington, Putney and Hounslow Cottage. Among Brown's patients in London was a drug-whacked Jimi Hendrix.

'I was a medical officer in Casualty at St Mary Abbott's Hospital in Kensington, 1970. Jimi Hendrix was brought in from an ambulance on a stretcher, dead. His girlfriend was there but nothing could be done.'

At the same hospital Brown recalls another incident where, 'at the same time in Casualty a film was being shot with Richard Burton and, to get to a critically ill patient, I walked straight across the set: annoying the producer no end'.

However, these flirtations with fame didn't hold great interest for Brown, who dedicated much of his time to work and self-education. He attempted a speed-reading course at an establishment just off Oxford Street—and managed to fail. He mused that because his speed-reading level was lower after the completion of the course than it had been when he began, had he stayed on he eventually would have been left illiterate.

There was a real opening up going on, as he developed some social networks. In modern terms he had his 'gaydar' working. The way Bob expresses it is that he found people who 'had the new attitude. A lot of the people I talked to weren't gay themselves, but they were comfortable with it. Just to be able to go beyond the psychologists and talk to other people about it was just terrific.'

It was an exciting time to be working in the middle of London. He found himself sharing a room with five other guys in a Kensington boarding house. His housemates were all straight, but there was a level of closeness and intimacy Bob so desperately needed. He swapped beds with a New Zealand fellow who had complained about bed bugs. As it turned out, the Kiwi got exactly the same bites from Bob's bed, while Bob remained immune.

Brown spent just over a year in England, including a side trip to Scotland with his mother Marjorie to witness the Commonwealth Games. It was also an opportunity to visit the ancestral home of Marjorie's family, the Frazers. He returned to Scotland solo on a later occasion to enjoy the snowy mountains and moors, armed only with a tent and sleeping bag. It was altogether building a newfound confidence within himself.

Immersion in London culture was undoubtedly vital in shaping a new worldliness in the young doctor. In the London hospitals he treated many people with drug-related conditions, as well as alcoholics and homeless people. The distance from home gave Brown a chance to reflect on his place in the world, and sharpened his resolve and commitment to working for social change when he returned to Australia.

❧ ❧ ❧

London had enabled Brown to come out of his shell on his own terms. Having spent just over two years abroad, his real political turning point began when he went to Tasmania. 'That was when I really fell on my feet,' he says.

Bob had taken a job as medical officer on a ship back to Sydney from London. Just before leaving London he was offered a job in Canberra at a practice with a turnover above $50,000 a year, with no outlay required from him. At first he wrote accepting the offer, then after deliberating, Brown decided that he wanted to keep his options open. He wrote a second letter, declining the position.

He arrived in Launceston in May 1972 to do a six-week locum as a GP. He recalls driving across the green countryside, looking at Mount Roland and the Central Plateau, and feeling an immediate 'topographical and vegetational connection' to the Tasmanian landscape, with its rocky peaks, alpine lakes and ancient forests.

'I'm no doubt a romantic in many ways, but this was romantic countryside,' he says. Bob had a strong sense that Tasmania was 'appropriate to me as a person and I guess my background'. The six-week locum passed and Bob was offered a permanent position in the Launceston surgery.

Just a few days after his arrival in Tasmania he wrote a postcard to his parents saying: 'I'm home'.

'It had something to do, I'm sure, with my background at Trunkey [Creek] and Glen Innes where you get a similar climate. I'd become involved in looking after the bush, along with many others, simply because I recognise how indescribably important and irreplaceable it is, both as a resource for we human beings and as a part of that life force which is so fascinating to me but which has a right to exist of its own accord.'

What followed were many camping trips into the Tasmanian wilderness, including to the Walls of Jerusalem. He joined a

Launceston bushwalking group. During those bush outings, people were talking about conservation issues which struck a deep chord with the young GP. It was also the first time Brown had been struck so squarely by the contrast between the beauty of wilderness and the destruction wreaked on it by human hands.

'I can clearly remember some of those early trips I took,' he says. 'One of the real eye-openers came on the first day I came to Tasmania. Among the extraordinary beauty of the Great Western Tiers and the highland country [was] the Great Lake [which] in those days had all these dead spars sticking out of it—hundreds of dead trees.'

'So, on the very first day I came to Tasmania I was struck by that contrast in the highland country. I remember taking photos of those dead trees; I couldn't believe it. The Hydro-Electric Commission had raised the Great Lake in the '60's, which had drowned all the lakeside trees . . . They were like so many skeletons sticking out of the water.'

One of the main reasons Bob Brown had originally been drawn to Tasmania was to search for the thylacine—also known as the Tasmanian tiger.

He had been fascinated by the thylacine since childhood. 'I believe when I came looking for the tiger it was extinct, in all probability, but there we were 36 years from the last known tiger, which died in Hobart Zoo in September 1936. Every year that passed made any chances of its survival, if it did exist, all the more difficult.'

As it had for many Tasmanians, the extinction of the thylacine—brought about at the hands of early Tasmanian farmers, government officials and bounty hunters—was a motivating factor in developing an environmental conscious-ness, a recognition that nature is precious and vulnerable to human destructiveness and mismanagement. Moreover, the thylacine became a deeply entrenched symbol in the Tasmanian consciousness that moved a new breed of conservationists to ensure the mistakes of the past weren't repeated.

David Owen, the Tasmanian author of the book *Thylacine: The tragic tale of the Tasmanian tiger*, agrees that the fate of the animal was certainly a factor in politicising Brown. 'Without a doubt,' says Owen. 'Tasmania's record of environmental trashing—never mind near-genocide—created the United Tasmania Group, and then the Tasmanian Wilderness Society, founded by Bob and others. The loss of the tiger is almost impossible to summarise and Bob has done profound things to change the world's attitude to the environment. The tiger's demise may just have started it.'

Brown joined a team of thylacine hunters who launched the state's biggest ever search. James O'Malley, a real estate agent from Smithton in north-west Tasmania, and Jeremy Griffith, a Sydney zoologist, began their search in 1968, four years before Brown was to join them. When Brown came to Launceston in 1972, he agreed to assist them by organising their Launceston-based information centre.

It was through Brown's work on the thylacine search that he first came in contact with a young radio journalist working at 7LA in Launceston, Peter Thompson. 'I have this clear recollection of recording an interview with him at the information centre about his thylacine search with Jeremy Griffith and James O'Malley,' says Thompson. 'We became friends pretty much straight away—he was interested in a range of things I was interested in, like the fate of Lake Pedder. I'm not even sure if that interview was broadcast, but Bob Brown was among the first people I interviewed.'

Thompson had noticed a small advertisement Brown had placed in the Launceston *Examiner* warning that the tiger had been driven to extinction by man's ignorance, and Lake Pedder could be next. Thompson says he was quite taken by this philosophical young doctor, who constantly talked about needing to make space for himself to do some serious writing.

'We used to have quite philosophical talks about what we'd like to do with our lives, and we were both quite committed to having some impact on the world for change. From those conversations, it was clear that he was interested in politics, but was much more of the mind to being an activist, rather than a politician,' says Thompson.

A great friendship and activist working relationship would develop between the two men over the next decade, ultimately leading to Thompson writing the book *Bob Brown of the Franklin River* in 1985.

Needless to say, after many trips into the bush, and a few instances when he believed for a moment he might have in fact sighted the elusive thylacine, Brown resigned himself that perhaps it was, after all, extinct. Or at least if it did exist, he wasn't going to be able to find it.

As Owen points out, Brown was the most skeptical of the team of thylacine hunters. Brown attributes his caution to six years of medicine, and a few other myth-shattering experiences he had behind him by then, resulting in a well-developed analytical mind. His companions, Griffiths and O'Malley, were 'glistening-eyed believers'.

Brown also told Owen he believes 'authorities' such as particular scientists and police have been complicit in perpetuating the myth of the tiger's existence by not exercising appropriate scientific rigour to their investigations of reported sightings. Moreover, Brown believes today that the chances of the tiger's existence are remote, in part because the predatorial history of the animal would make it difficult for it to survive the adjustment to being viewed as vermin. He is also skeptical of moves attempting to clone the thylacine spearheaded by the Australian Museum. 'It's addle-brained to think that you can recreate tigers without protecting their habitat,' says Brown. 'At the moment, the Tasmanian Government are sprinkling 1080 [a poison used to deter wildlife from eating tree seedlings planted after forest clearfelling] all over it. The idea of cloning is the absurdity of thinking that humankind can purchase environments off the shelf, and can purchase ingredients off the shelf. And it aint so, it just isn't so.'

But for Brown's part, in the early 1970s the search for the elusive thylacine was nevertheless a worthwhile endeavour, and marked a critical period of rationalism and scientific enquiry, which also strengthened his connection to the Tasmanian wilderness and the burgeoning environmental movement. It was, too, a profound early template, illustrating the need for environmental defenders in Tasmania and the world at large—a quest that stirred Bob Brown from a child-hood fascination with the tiger to an adult revelation about the frailty of nature at the hands of humans.

Thompson says that while the tiger search may have been the 'excuse' for Brown's coming to Tasmania, he believes Bob 'may well have found some other reason to go to Tasmania and investigate. It may well have been Lake Pedder. The pull of the place, whatever it was, got him there in the first place. He was still wrestling with what he was going to do with his life . . . and Tasmania is transfixing.'

❧ ❧ ❧

On 17 November 1973, Bob Brown cemented his connection with Tasmania by purchasing a bush block at Liffey, in Tasmania's central north, for $8000. He had heard the property was for sale, and that a fella named John Dean was on the lookout for a buyer. When he went to see Dean, how-ever, Brown was told that the property had just been sold to a young couple in the last few days. Believing himself out of luck, he liked the property so much that he left his number with Dean regardless, just in case.

Within a couple of days, Dean rang Brown to inform him that the previous buyer's wife had taken one look at the weather-board house and rambling bushlands around it and put a stop to the transaction. Bob jumped at the opportunity.

He was 28 years old. He still owns the bush block in the Liffey Valley today and by the look of it, not much has changed in the intervening thirty years.

A sign on the front gate reads 'Trespassers Welcome: No Guns'.

The picture-book beautiful 27-acre block, which borders on the Liffey Falls Reserve and the Great Western Tiers Conservation Area, has a section of the Liffey River running right through it. Reaching 1340 metres into the sky behind the property are the razorback ridges of Drys Bluff. A few metres higher than Mount Wellington (1270 metres), the bluff is snow-capped in the winter months.

Two wild white ponies graze the grassy area in front of a simple white weatherboard house perched by itself in the middle of the block. In its simplicity and austerity, Bob Brown's Liffey house looks a little like a church. The place is made up of a master bedroom at the front eastern side, a smaller study on the western frontage, with a fair-sized kitchen and sunroom behind them. The sounds of the trickling water from the Liffey River, as well as the background flutter of birds overhead, are constantly discernible from the front porch of the four-roomed timber dwelling.

There is no power or telephone access.

In the study at the front, a modest bookshelf gives a clue as to a lifetime of sparse reading. Besides the staples of *Roget's Thesaurus* and the *Oxford Concise Dictionary*, there are numerous conservation books including Paddles' *The Last Tasmanian Tiger*, Suzuki's *Inventing the Future* and several books on Lake Pedder. There are also numerous books here on poetry and writing and several compilations of famous quotations. Besides that, it is difficult to find any real pattern to the books—Jung's *Memories, Dreams, Reflections* sits beside a book on flower and plant identification in Tasmania. The top row houses more recent acquisitions—Martin Flanagan's *In Sunshine or in Shadow*, Henry Reynolds' *This Whispering in our Hearts*, John Ralston Saul's *The Unconscious Civilization*, and Mohammad Mohaddessin's *Islamic Fundamentalism— The New Global Threat.*

The study is adorned with framed pictures, mainly nature shots of local waterfalls and mountains that Bob has taken and had enlarged. Other images include a 1923 water-colour painting by Jack Keates of crowds cheering besides a river, entitled 'The Liffey Swim'. Another picture shows three people doing handstands on the now-drowned Lake Pedder beach.

The pictorial adornments continue throughout the entire house. In the kitchen, most of the framed pictures are of Bob's mother and father, Jack and Marjorie. There is also a recent photo of Bob and his partner since 1996, Paul Thomas, standing arm in arm. Next to the toilet in the small bathroom out back, a cut-out quote from Oscar Wilde reads: 'In olden times they used to have the rack, now they've got the press'.

Only a few metres behind the house the grassland gives way to the wild forest and the razorback rocky outcrops of Drys Bluff. Just a stone's throw behind the house, the paddock lands disappear into a winding path leading into the heart of the forest, a mix of wet sclerophyll and cool temperate rainforest.

This is beautiful regrowth forest, logged back in the early 1900s, with the original rainforest understorey of *Pittosporum* and forest ferns now re-establishing itself. The wild whites and yellows of flowering *Delegatensis*, *Obliqua* and *Viminalis* stand alongside the towering sassafras, dogwood, white gum, brown top, myrtle and other eucalypt trees.

The path winds through the trees to a clearing that looks as though it could be a secret meeting point nestled in the forest proper.

The roads around Liffey curve and wind though grassy properties and forested valleys, crisscrossing the Liffey River. The picture book calm is only disturbed by the log trucks that routinely thunder along these roads, an ever-present reminder of the nature of the challenges that have occupied the mind of Bob Brown since he settled here in 1974.

'When . . . you've got a mountain at the back reminding you of the wilderness, and you've got log trucks constantly rolling down the street, it does confront you,' says Brown. 'It helps you to realise you do have the power to change things.'

The shock of Pedder

Chapter 5

From the time Brown arrived in Tasmania in mid-1972, he had watched intently as the battle for Lake Pedder played out.

Although never directly involved in the thick of the campaign to save Pedder, Brown says the shock of seeing those in power walk over the arguments of conservationists was a significant motivator in politicising a whole new batch of conservationists, including himself, for the battles that lay ahead.

From the day he commenced his initial locum at the Launceston surgery in May 1972, Brown had noticed a group of people who had set up a caravan in Launceston drawing attention to the government's plans to flood Lake Pedder. 'The Lake Pedder people arrived with their caravan in Launceston and I quickly fell in with them,' he says.

Through this initial contact with the Lake Pedder campaign, toward which Brown began donating some of his doctor's wages, he met many people who he would later come to work with through years of environmental campaigning.

But there were many other instances of Bob Brown's taking proactive personal steps toward political immersion throughout this period. He had come back from London with a new energy for social change, and a confidence he had never before known in his own ability for cultural engagement and political transformation.

What transpired was a period of metamorphoses—a process begun in England—with Brown spending a good proportion of his time and doctor's wages taking the fateful first steps down a path that would lead to a life of political and environmental activism.

He took out advertisements in the national and Tasmanian press under the headline 'Tasmania—World Epitome of Man's Destructiveness', detailing a history of disgraces on the island, from the genocide of the Aboriginal population to the flooding of Lake Pedder. In the advertisement he appended the date of the death of the last Tasmanian Aboriginal Truganini in 1876, with the caption, 'The only successful deliberate annihilation of any whole human race in history'. The advertisement also detailed how the Tasmanian Government had in 1888 offered a £1 bounty on the thylacine, followed by the word 'Slaughter'.

At the bottom of the advertisement, in reference to the events unfolding around Lake Pedder, Brown wrote 'The Tradition Lives on . . .'.

The Launceston *Examiner* traced the source of the advertisements, which appeared in the three Tasmanian papers and the *Australian* signed only R.J.B, to Brown in his suburban Launceston surgery. The *Examiner*'s editorial commentary wrote of Brown: 'He doesn't expect anything in return for his $1000 investment . . . except satisfaction. But he hopes it will make planners stop and think a little more before making decisions that affect the environment . . . Bob Brown could be leading the good life on the substantial salary of a doctor . . .'

Even at this early stage, Bob Brown was mystifying the press.

When Gough Whitlam came to Launceston airport in 1972, he was met by a rather incongruous-looking young doctor in a three-piece suit holding a placard saying 'Ban Uranium Sales'. 'And then,' recalls Brown, 'having caught his eye there, I hurried into town in my car, parked it, and went and stood in front of the main hotel in Launceston and felt a real fool, but I was determined to make myself do it'.

Brown's resolve that Australia should not be going down the 'yellowcake' road was to be something that would galvanise him for decades to come. The nuclear issue, and the idea of a nuclear winter, was a fear that would keep Brown awake at night. Peter Thompson and Bob Brown had developed quite a strong friendship, and Thompson says he can clearly remember Bob being 'almost obsessed' by the growing nuclear threat.

'I remember his being quite affected by Nixon raising the global nuclear alert to amber,' says Thompson. 'This was the time when there was a lot of pressure on Nixon over Watergate. I remember Bob being terribly affected by it. He was constantly asking questions like, "How will the world be?" "How will we survive a nuclear winter?" He was . . . exercised by this deployment of nuclear weapons and the threat to life through nuclear armaments. I can't imagine many people in the world at that time sharing concern to that extent, not about just that issue, but about the fundamental injustices of the world and the excesses of military power—these things were keeping Bob awake night after night, dominating his mind.'

'Those age-old philosophical questions—how should I live, what should I think and do? It went round and round [in] his head—what must I do? From the early days he took very seriously the notion that he had a personal responsibility—he had to do something about the state of the world,' says Thompson.

On another occasion, the recently incumbent Prime Minister Malcolm Fraser paid a visit to Launceston, and had a luncheon with locals almost across the road from the surgery. Brown left his appointment book blank for the afternoon, determined to converse with the nation's prime minister on an issue of utmost importance. 'I . . . asked him what he thought the chances of a nuclear war and everybody being killed were,' recalls Brown.

'His reply was along the lines of, "Well, it's likely", and I further inquired as to why aren't we doing more about this, and he was quite perplexed. I was actually taken by the humanness of his answer,' said Brown.

It wouldn't be the last time Fraser would hear from Bob Brown.

When the USS *Enterprise* aircraft carrier came to Hobart in November 1976, Bob Brown staged a fast in the rain and hail on the peak of Mount Wellington, attracting national media attention to his conviction that Tasmania—and, indeed, the rest of Australia—should not be welcoming US warships to its ports. His feat was a highly theatrical gesture that, even more successfully than his previous advertisements, attracted the interest of the nation's media.

The Launceston *Examiner* noted Brown's action in its editorial on 10 November, praising Dr Brown of Liffey for getting his message across 'without a vestige of anti-Americanism or political hypocrisy'. Letters of support were printed in the paper, including one from David Murphy of Legana, who wrote, 'The lonely vigil of Doctor Brown on the summit of Mt Wellington as a protest against the visit of the nuclear-powered USS Enterprise speaks for thousands of concerned people throughout the world. This concern is not expressed in the strident voice of anti-Americanism or political extremism, but is a genuine fear for the future of mankind in a nuclear powered world.'

Brown's actions had not only drawn media interest; he was already rallying parts of the Tasmanian public behind him.

In April 1977, Brown would make his first political address to a small 100-strong rally in Launceston, as an active member of the local branch of the Australian Uranium Moratorium Group (AUMG). By that stage, he was also putting together AUMG press releases, and in some cases hand-delivering them to Tasmanian newspaper offices.

In July that same year Brown again addressed an anti-nuclear rally in Launceston, this time outside the office of the then federal minister for Environment, Kevin Newman. Brown suggested in his speech that unless the minister opposed Australia's nuclear involvement, he wasn't in fact the minister for Environment. He was the minister against the environment. Brown struck the right note and drew rapturous applause from the 1500-strong crowd.

❧ ❧ ❧

But it was outrage around the Lake Pedder flooding, more than any other issue, that galvanised Bob Brown into political action. Indeed, the Lake Pedder campaign is often pointed to as the primary catalyst behind the formation of the world's first Green party, the United Tasmania Group. 'I'd come at the end of Lake Pedder and for me it was a great learning experience and it was frightening and it was awesome and it was a great sense of tragedy,' says Brown.

'I'd seen an ABC *Four Corners* program on Lake Pedder before I came to Tasmania, so it interested me straight up. In May 1972 I flew over the lake with a couple of other doctors. I remember there were small rainstorms happening in some places, then sun coming up in other places. That interplay of light and shade was a beautiful picture through the clouds, I still remember that clearly today.'

Lake Pedder was a sub-alpine aquatic environment, described by UNESCO as 'a unique wilderness of incomparable significance and value', and its imminent flooding derided as 'the greatest ecological tragedy since European settlement in Tasmania'. It was a base for early wilderness explorers in Tasmania's south-west, dating well back into last century. By March 1955, following submissions on the value of the area by the Hobart Walkers Club, an area of 24 000 hectares around Pedder was set aside as national park.

However, what was not revealed was that as early as 1953, the Hydro-Electric Commission had installed flow-recorders in the region. In 1963 the state government sought funding to put a road into the heart of the south-west Pedder region, and in June 1965 then Tasmanian premier Eric Reece conceded that there was to be 'some modification' to the Lake Pedder National Park.

During his initial six-week locum in Launceston Brown had hired a small plane to see Pedder for himself. He describes the lake in his writings in this way: 'The park protected a lake shaped ten thousand years earlier by the retreating Ice Age. Lake Pedder was unique. Set at an altitude of 300 metres and surrounded by mountains, it had a three kilometre beach made of fine, pink, quartzite sand and was the habitat for rare plants and aquatic species, including the native trout *Galaxias pedderensis*.'

Environmentalists were incensed by the recognition that up to seventeen species would perish if the flooding of the lake were to go ahead. Moreover, the government planned to inundate the lake to a depth of more than 15 metres, with only the top few metres being drawn off for power production, meaning that the remaining 97 per cent would become dead storage.

As early as May 1967 the Tasmanian Government announced its plans to the state parliament—Lake Pedder would be drowned out by dams on the Huon and Serpentine rivers, resulting in an impoundment of nearly 250 square kilometres of water.

Despite the gathering of Tasmania's biggest ever petition at the time of 10 000 signatures opposing the plans, despite a packed-to-the-rafters public meeting at Hobart Town Hall in 1971 calling for a referendum, despite an independent poll carried out by the independent *Saturday Evening Mercury* newspaper which noted 1172 against and 37 for, despite condemnation from UNESCO of the plans, despite the signatures of 184 international scientists voicing their dissent, by July 1972 Pedder beach had disappeared.

'I heard one or two people saying that they had really been too soft, that there should have been direct action, and they were talking about violent direct action,' says Brown. 'It was just this anguish that they should have blown up something, that something should have happened. They felt in a way, in amongst all the other emotions, a guilt that they hadn't . . . tried hard enough. Whereas in fact in the circumstances of the day they had created perhaps the first great land environment campaign in modern Australian history.'

Although Brown may not have agreed with some of the more extreme sentiments expressed after the loss of Pedder, he was clearly moved by this new breed of conservationists, and their astute tenacity in articulating the value and wonder of nature. 'It wasn't until I came to Tasmania and met the young turks of the South-West Tasmanian Action Committee and the Lake Pedder campaign and then the early Wilderness Society; and heard them express the value of wilderness . . . in a way which rang true with me, which I had in my head but hadn't been able to express, that I was free to do the same. The curious business of learning from people younger than yourself, how to express something that was extraordinarily important.'

Brown says the actions around Pedder, although unsuccessful in the end, 'certainly . . . set the template for saving the Franklin'.

'I was aware of that and that history was a great strength. The other thing it taught us, while we were getting our pictures for the Franklin River, was that [pictures weren't] enough. There were plenty of pictures of Lake Pedder but at the end of the day the Hydro would just walk over and, like a foot on a walnut, squash your arguments flat if you hadn't got an economic and employment argument to put back to them.'

Brown says he was fortunate not to be in the thick of the Lake Pedder campaign. 'People were really rolled over by the might and the obsequiousness of the HEC and the Reece Government. I was hearing about what was going on, and there was a sense of despairing—but I was busy in other areas. The ad in the paper did have a component of despair about the absurdity of it. The big image in my mind was Lake Pedder— not the dam works, not the bulldozers.'

However, an event occurred which remains unresolved today. Max Price and Brenda Hean had been two of the principal opponents of the Pedder development. In a last-ditch effort to draw national media attention, the pair had set off from Hobart at 10.16 a.m. on Friday 8 September 1972 in a World War I Tiger Moth on a mission to skywrite over Canberra their opposition to the Pedder development.

Brenda had received a mysterious phone call several days before the ill-fated flight asking if she was prepared to give up now that the legal challenges had failed. She answered that she wasn't, and that 'There is still plenty we can do yet'. The male caller said, 'Mrs Hean, how would you like to go for a swim?' before hanging up.

It was later discovered that the side door of the hangar from which the plane left had been broken open with an axe on the night before the plane's departure. The high-impact search beacon that could have been used to help rescuers locate the plane crash was hidden behind some crates at the back of the hangar. The Reece Government refused to appoint a royal commission to investigate the Pedder campaigners' disappearance.

Brown says he learnt a sobering lesson from the events around Lake Pedder.

'I learnt that you've got to be tough in return, even if it's not in your nature. You see it all the time in the forest campaigns now—the really good-hearted people getting crunched in the middle because they want to resolve the issue.'

'People were terrified after that,' says Brown, 'I remember people saying they'd heard about the death threat, and after that they were afraid to get up in the morning and put their foot on the accelerator for fear the car would blow up. Those people really believed the world was a decent place, and a bit more reason here would fix it—but of course it doesn't.'

❧ ❧ ❧

The seemingly senseless destruction of Pedder, and the events that surrounded it, had an enormous impact on motivating a new environment movement, and its rising leader. National newspapers were starting to take notice of the conservationists' arguments.

In the *Age* editorial of 25 October 1972, the paper noted, 'In the future, Australians will be more ready to fight for their environment . . . the Australian people have come to a new and marked awareness of the environment and the importance of preserving it. Conservation may have been a mere catch-cry a few years ago; it is no longer . . . One Lake Pedder tragedy is one too many.'

Prime Minister Gough Whitlam offered the Tasmanian Reece Labor Government \$8.8 million to finance a moratorium on the project, work on which was already well under way. The Tasmanian caucus rejected the offer in mid-November 1973. 'Death by drowning was the sentence passed on Pedder by the Tasmanian government,' pronounced the *Age* on 16 November.

Christine Milne, former Tasmanian Greens leader and current adviser to Bob Brown and Oceania Councillor to the World Conservation Union, says Pedder was the watershed event that 'radicalised' her, and many other Tasmanian environmental activists into political activism.

'I was at uni at the time, I wasn't active before that. I thought it would be saved and then when it wasn't I determined that the next time around I would be involved. It was really the loss of Lake Pedder that radicalised a lot of people for the Franklin campaign,' she says. 'That can be seen in the polarisation that occurred out of the Franklin issue—it was Tasmania challenging the excesses that were occurring with the onset of industrialisation. It got to the point where we said the damage of industrialisation on the environment cannot be tolerated and we're taking a stand.'

Bob Brown was also clearly moved enough by the events around Pedder to devote much of his time, energy and wages toward environmental activism from that time forth. 'I'd put a bit of money into that [Lake Pedder] campaign, both directly into it and publicising it.'

This was before the rise of US environmental groups such as Earth First!, before the idea of environmental activism had entered the global consciousness. These were pioneering days, and Tasmania was a precursor to what would become a defining movement of the late twentieth century.

The timing couldn't have been more fortuitous in motivating a young GP who already had his own environmental and political leanings, and who was looking for a solid philosophical foundation and direction. Cassandra Pybus, a sixth-generation Tasmanian academic, concurs that the Green movement in Australia was born when Pedder disappeared.

'What was mourned and derided as a loss and failure has, in time, become a political metaphor of considerable power,' wrote Pybus.

> Pedder may have been lost in those early days and the Green Party it spawned [the United Tasmania Group] may have failed to get any seats in parliament, but the campaign inspired a whole clutch of activists, many of whom are dominant figures in Green politics today. The Pedder furore threw up individuals of remarkable perserverance and commitment who continue to be an inspiration around the world.

In the space of just a few years, Bob Brown had completed a remarkable metamorphosis. He had completed a shift in his identity from that of a confused, repressed and extremely shy medical student whose politics seemed more closely aligned with conservatives. The young GP was now involving himself, in a highly public and political fashion, in conservation battles that would come to be viewed as pioneering in the birth of the Greens globally. Moreover, he was emerging as a leader among the conservationists.

The link between Pedder and the United Tasmania Group is a clear and personal one for many. Christine Milne went so far as to say 'the failure of Lake Pedder was needed in a way'. She was speaking of the shock of seeing Pedder disappear and its resulting political impetus—that ordinary Tasmanians would no longer sit back and watch their state's environmental beauty destroyed by economic interests.

It is generally claimed that the birth of the Greens occurred in March 1972 when Richard Jones formed the United Tasmania Group (UTG). This view appears to be generally accepted by Greens themselves (it went unchallenged at the Global Greens conference in 2001), but it should be noted that there are voices within the broader Australian conservation movement who would question its accuracy.

William J. Lines, author of *Taming the Great South Land: A History of the Conquest of Nature in Australia*, wrote in *Quarterly Essay* in 2003 that there were earlier precedents. 'In February 1971 three members of the Colong Committee—including Milo Dunphy—stood as Australia Party candidates in the New South Wales elections. Their platforms were specifically conservationist,' he says.

Lines describes the theory that the UTG was the world's first Green party as 'folklore' and 'untrue'. However, given the acceptance of the UTG as the party's forebear among Greens themselves, and the similarity of the UTG's charter to that of the party that later became the Australian Greens, it is fair to say that the UTG was a primary catalyst for the global Green political movement.

Christine Milne describes this moment of burgeoning green consciousness as having been the moment of 'radicalisation' on a personal level for many. 'The fact is that the world's first Green party was formed here as a result of Pedder, the second Green Party in New Zealand shortly thereafter, and then Petra Kelly taking that ethos to Europe and establishing the German Greens. So the whole global Green movement started here in Tasmania as a result of environmentalism challenging the industrial paradigm.'

The UTG formed out of the realisation that economic industrialisation could be victorious over environmental and community values, as evidenced by the flooding of Lake Pedder and the hunting of the thylacine to its extinction. The UTG realised that direct engagement with the political structure was absolutely necessary in order to prevent that course from proceeding unchecked.

The new environmental and political ethic articulated by the UTG in March 1972 included in its charter that the group was 'united in a global movement for survival', 'condemn[s] the misuse of power for individual or group prominence', and sought to 'create new means of community participation in government'. These principles may seem common enough goals today, but at the time they were radical and unprecedented—potent principles for profound political change. They flew directly in the face of established party politics, both in Tasmania and the world, and became an early catalyst for a massively influential global movement.

Bob Brown was keeping a close eye on the emergence of the UTG. Richard Jones—cited by Bob Brown as one of his key influences—articulated in his 1973 essay 'A New Movement for Social and Political Change' many of the ideas that would become platforms for the global Green movement.

A hierarchical society of the sort ours is, or the sort that Russia is, cannot provide humane solutions to the ecology problem. We are obliged to create a political and social movement that does not distinguish between politicians as the rulers and the rest of us as the ruled . . . The degree to which we fail to create a new ecological movement will be the degree to which we are destined to move towards a rigid dictatorship founded on the developing techniques of 'resource management'. That is why the creation of such a movement matters, and why, if it fails, the extent of its failure matters.

Jones also presaged the problem of dogmatism versus pragmatism that still troubles Green parties the world over today.

> Environmental militants should not cut themselves off from the present ecology lobby, the trade union movement, or from political parties. The idea is not primarily to get these organisations to adopt the strategies we advocate, but rather to raise doubts and spread ideas. It is important to move people to halfway to where they should be, because they'll never get all the way unless they come halfway first.

The formation of the UTG and the Tasmanian Greens didn't go unnoticed by people around the world. Richard Jones could not have realised the potency of his message. But, perhaps more than any other, this was the moment of inception for the Greens—a political party now recognised and represented in every continent of the world, and whose global political leverage we are only today seeing blossom nationally in Australia.

The UTG also saw Bob Brown make his debut as a political candidate. Brown's first political charge was met with a rather humbling response. On the back of the dismissal of the Whitlam Government in 1975, Brown ran as a second stringer on the UTG ticket to the Australian Senate. At one point on the election night, as voting figures for the major parties soared into the thousands, Brown's tally was just two votes. By the end of the election his votes had climbed into triple figures. But then he had never expected to win the seat.

As the following years have borne out, Bob Brown was going to do what he could to follow his still developing philosophical convictions. He was quickly getting a name for himself as an outspoken Launceston doctor, not afraid to make his concerns very public. In a precursor to the 'Reclaim the Streets' and 'Critical Mass' bike rallies that still continue all over the world today, in 1977 Bob Brown was lobbying the Launceston City Council to build more bike paths.

Brown himself had used bicycles for years as his preferred mode of transport to work in Launceston from his home in Liffey, but he wanted the council to include a bikeway in its planning for new northern roadworks out of Launceston. He door-knocked the area to ascertain whether residents were in favour of the idea (they were). He then developed a 16-page submission to the city council detailing the logistics of the project.

In April 1977 a massive bike rally was organised. Participants rode into Launceston in a blaze of colour. The rally was addressed by the town's mayor, who relayed the news that the council was willing to work with the bikeway committee toward setting up the new bike paths.

Brown's poor electoral debut did nothing to weaken his resolve. In September 1976, fresh from his first rafting trip down the Franklin, Brown wrote a piece for the UTG newsletter that bore testament to his transformation to a homespun conservationist philosophy.

Here he articulated his own politicisation:

Selfishness prevails on Earth. Nowhere is this more apparent than in Australia. We live for maximising personal wealth and ignore the miseries of our neighbours; we plunder our natural resources as if we are the most deserving generation that has ever been or ever will be; we rush to gain advantage from technological innovation even when there are appalling risks; we claim parenthood as a joyous right but leach the joy from our children's futures. As a result mankind faces a needlessly wretched future. At best there will be prolonged repression, cruelty and hate until reason gains ascendancy in a human community desperate for happiness. At worst human life will cease at its own hand.

Armed with that kind of puissant awareness, Bob Brown was ready to take on anything. He had passed the point of no return.

Franklin daze Chapter 6

If the flooding of Lake Pedder was the watershed event for the birth of the world's first Green party and the politicisation of Bob Brown, the Franklin was the issue that thrust those politics—and indeed Brown himself—directly into the national media spotlight.

When forester Paul Smith invited Brown to take a trip with him rafting the Franklin, he couldn't have had any inkling what a profoundly instrumental journey it would be. The two-week rafting trip Brown and Smith undertook on a clear sunny day in February 1976 has today taken on the mythic proportions of an odyssey. It is the oft-recounted journey of discovery, considered the starting point for a campaign that would stretch over six years and come to arrest the attention of an entire nation.

Bob Brown made a deal with Paul Smith. Smith would accompany Brown on a bushwalk to the Western Arthurs, a mountain range in the state's south-west, on the proviso that Brown would then join him on a rafting trip down the

Franklin. 'He was a bit desperate for somebody to go with him,' says Brown.

So the pair set off from the Collingwood Bridge with rubber rafts, waterproofed sleeping bags, a tent and camera gear, and inflatable lilos and pillows for comfort. They kept food supplies in rucksacks, had several metres of strong rope, life jackets, and rubber-soled boots.

Today the Collingwood Bridge, which crosses the Collingwood River on the Lyell Highway between Queenstown and Hamilton, is a popular set-off point for whitewater rafters. However, a sign in the car park beside the river emphatically warns: 'This is not a place to learn White Water skills. This river system is dangerous. Several people have died while travelling on it.'

No such warnings greeted Brown and Smith in their expedition, although they were not the first to set about the journey. In December 1951, John Hawkins, Jo Scarlett, Jeff Weston, and John Dean (from whom Brown bought his Liffey property) set out on the first recorded trip down the Franklin. They were travelling in 5-metre, 50-kg ex-army float boats. The group's trip ended in calamity when John Hawkins was knocked unconscious after being thrown from the boat on Descension Gorge. They walked the last 30 kilometres of the trip.

The group returned in 1958 to try again, this time in fibreglass canoes. John Dean was reported as saying, 'I got such a hell of a scare it took that long to get over it'. However, this second journey was also called off when Dean's boat was smashed in two on rocks. Unwilling to quit, the group returned the next summer and completed the journey. They were picked up at the Gordon River below the Franklin by tour operator Reg Morrison in his boat the *J. Lee M.*

Sir Edmund Hillary described the south-west Tasmania wilderness as 'one of the last great wilderness areas of the world'. The Franklin River, as author James McQueen noted, is different from other rivers. 'There was no detergent in its waters, no heavy metals or sewage; there were no beer cans or broken bottles or old iron in its bed, there were no black-berries on its banks, no ragwort or willows; there were no sparrows or rabbits, no bridges or culverts or boat ramps.'

The Franklin is one of the last wild, unchanged rivers in the world.

When Brown contemplated the journey, his primary worry was the possibility of rafting equipment failure. 'I had visions of this [trip] being interfered with by failed technology; that is, patching up tubes and patching up rafts and fiddling around with gear all the way,' says Brown.

'I'm a bit impatient with that sort of thing; I'd like to be getting on and enjoying the bush. But it didn't turn out that way. In fact, I think we had a puncture each and that was it. We did have a lot of gear, we did have to take a lot of food, and there was a lot of heaving and hauling—but the gear went exceptionally well,' recalls Brown.

Smith, the more experienced rafter of the two, had his own agenda for the trip. He wanted to see for himself if the rumours about the intentions of the Hydro-Electric Commission (HEC) were true—he would be scouring for flood-lines along the shores of the Franklin and Lower Gordon.

For Brown's part, he was more interested in simply lapping up the natural environment. He was to speak later of the capacity of the river to instil in him a new kind of self, 'something better than exists in the everyday world'. Brown can reel off a plethora of memories and impressions of that trip. 'First of all, the wonderful weather, but coming to the Irenabyss and camping there and then floating back up into it. It was just wonderful.'

'And down the Engineer Range which gradually got bigger and bigger and bigger and then finally into the Great Ravine itself, and camping in there and wondering if it rained how we'd get out, and what was coming further down. Getting through to the end of that and camping at the far end, coming across the Huon pines below the Loddon River, and knowing we were through.'

'It was exhilarating . . . you'd see a big cliff face starting to come into focus behind the right-hand side of a group of tall eucalypts or riverside trees, myrtles, down some hundreds of metres. [Then] this cliff face would float more and more into view and you knew there'd be rapids under it. It was a wonderful feeling.'

Brown was only 31 years old, and would have needed all the youthful vitality he could muster. But one thing that comes through is Brown's fearlessness of the river, despite his inexperience. There are stories of later rafting expeditions where Brown rafted some of the most difficult parts of the river without a life jacket for protection.

Throughout the years that followed, many conservationists from all over Australia undertook journeys down the Franklin to join in the protests, but at the time Smith and Brown set out, such a trip was a rare event.

The reality of the perilousness of the trip hit home when, on the second bend, Smith and Brown passed a group of fishermen on the banks of the river. After Smith told them they were headed downstream to Strahan, one of the three fishermen informed them they were 'bloody mad' to be doing it.

Even to local fishermen, such a trip was hazardous in the extreme. But Smith and Brown weren't oblivious to the dangers. 'We had to be very careful and we were quite apprehensive about a lot of rapids because we simply didn't know,' says Brown.

They floated into an area called the Irenabyss where there was no visibility of exactly what lay ahead in the rapids. 'That was done a bit on spec—very exciting. Very silly when you think about it later on—we should have tried harder and we could have got out and had a look. But just wonderful to go through this rollicking set of rapids and suddenly spin out onto deep, almost still, flowing water between these cliffs with just a plink, plink, plink of a little drop of water here and there and moss on the sides and the curl of the white foam from the rapid above coming down in the middle of the stream. Quite magnificent,' says Brown.

The pair found beautiful campsites by the side of the river, and encountered few hindrances. At one point, Smith cut his arm after slipping on quartzite and fell down a 3-metre cliff. Luckily, doctor Brown was on hand, and quickly tended the bleeding wound. It was only later in the trip that Smith and Brown began noticing some unusual intrusions on the surrounding environs of the river. There beside the ebb and flow of the currents, diminishing the perfection of the pristine forest embankments: the unmistakeable signs of human intervention.

'It was a shock in mid-river to come across the Mount McCall haulage way where they had run a railway track down the side of a gorge which was to be dam no. 2, 200 metres high, below the Great Ravine . . . So it came as a real shock at the end to recognise that this was dinkum, that the money was being poured in here, that nobody knew about it and that this region within a few years was going to be lost. Very sobering stuff,' said Brown.

By the end of the trip, the pair had seen drills, barges, helicopters, and heard explosions. Clearly the Hydro-Electric Commission were there, and plans were already well under way to dam the Franklin. 'The full bit, as they were preparing the dam site then downstream at Butler Island for this first of a series of dams which was going to flood back up,' recalls Brown. 'Paul had maps and knew where the flood-lines would be, but I was too busy taking it all in to be looking at hypotheticals about dams and so on.'

❧ ❧ ❧

Bob Brown and Paul Smith weren't the first to have noticed the encroaching presence of the Hydro-Electric Commission on the Franklin. Reg Morrison had been a tour operator around the Gordon and Franklin rivers since the 1950s. He and his companions, including a tour operator named Deni

Hamill, had already made their feelings about any potential damming of the Franklin known to the HEC.

Deni Hamill, 64, had grown up in the west coast port town of Strahan in one of the largest families in the area. Hamill says Strahan had always been one of the busiest port towns in Tasmania. He can recall as a child the boats bringing in the coal, and taking away timber and copper. By the 1950s Strahan was the port that received shipments of Holden cars into Tasmania from the mainland.

Hamill had been a timber-cutter and boatbuilder before hooking up with tour operator Reg Morrison to work on the tourist boats. 'I worked on the *Denison Star* tourist boat,' he recalls. Hamill says his boss Reg Morrison used to insist on his boat operators talking to the tourists about the environmental value of the areas they were visiting, and Morrison had possessed a 'visionary' ecotourism perspective as early as the 1950s. 'Reg Morrison has been talking about ecotourism all his life,' says Hamill. 'There's always been tourism boats here in Strahan. There's always been boats taking piners up the rivers. But the *J. Lee M* was the first one to cart buses. She started in about 1954. He had her built especially to cart tourists on the Gordon.'

It wasn't long before the ecotourism vision came under direct threat from the Hydro-Electric Commission. 'We had fought HEC many years before the blockade came on,' says Hamill. 'They said they were going to build a dam somewhere in the Lower Gordon, just below the mouth of the Franklin River. Then they actually blocked off the river with a wire where we used to travel past, so we couldn't show the Hydro camps to the tourists. Then Reg cancelled all his contracts with the Hydro, so he wouldn't carry any supplies on the *Denison Star* or the barges he used to tow for them with the *J. Lee M*. That was probably the [precedent for] the whole blockade. Like Reg said: "To dam that river would be like cutting off the blood supply to my body". Don't worry—he meant it.'

As history would reveal, the 64-foot *J. Lee M*, which was named after Morrison's parents James and Lee Morrison, was also to become a vital component in the forthcoming blockade.

Brown and Smith completed their journey on 7 March 1976 with mixed emotions. The exhilaration of the wondrous expedition they had just completed was mingled with the trepidation of a poisonous new knowledge—that the HEC had similar designs on the Franklin as they had held in regard to Lake Pedder. There had been rumours circulating for some time, but the rumours were now transformed into acute awareness—the river was in perilous danger.

Having completed their rafting, Brown and Smith waited below the HEC camp at Butler Island for the passing tourist boat, the *Denison Star*, to pick them up and take them to Strahan. The skipper of the *Denison Star*, Reg Morrison, shared their fears about the HEC's plans for the river. Brown was also astounded to bump into John Dean, from whom he had purchased the Liffey property, on board the boat.

'There were connections all over the place,' he says. Aside from the coincidental connections, the group all expressed fear and outrage to one another that this beautiful environment was under such serious immediate threat. Reg Morrison and Deni Hamill were to play vital roles in the protest campaign over the coming years.

Hamill remembers this first meeting with Brown. 'He was immediately likeable, with an incredibly infectious personality.' Elated from the trip he had just taken, and confident in the course he was about to undertake in attempting to save the river, Brown made a marked impression on the crew of the *Denison Star*. He had come a long way from the shy confused young man of just five years before.

Bob Brown had become a man with a mission.

After that first trip, things moved fast. Paul Smith made a commitment at the end of the trip to return and document the Franklin in film. Later that year, the first meeting of a core group of sixteen conservationists gathered at Bob Brown's Liffey property to plan the beginnings of the Franklin campaign.

The group, which included Kevin Kiernan, Helen Gee and Paul Smith, decided to change the name of the organisation from the South-West Tasmanian Action Committee (SWTAC) to the Tasmanian Wilderness Society (TWS). Brown suggests one of the reasons for the name change was that SWTAC had been generating a lot of negative publicity, particularly in the Hobart *Mercury* newspaper, and following from the US Wilderness Society, the Tasmanian Wilderness Society seemed to have a more 'conservative' and 'staid' ring to it.

Brown says he is sure the Franklin campaign would have happened regardless of his Franklin trip with Paul Smith, but 'It's great fortune . . . that Paul pushed that trip so early on,' he says. 'And he wasn't just doing it for an outing. He had his flood-lines on those maps that we took down at that time . . . So, although he's not a campaigner as such, he was setting up this specific campaign in his mind, and his contribution to it. And it got us under way years before it would otherwise have happened . . . I think it was instrumental in such a close contest, at the end of the day, in saving it.'

Fellow environmental activist and writer Helen Gee had her own stories to tell at the Liffey meeting. She and others had recently been down the Jane River into the lower Franklin on lilos, and had made their own observations of the movements of the HEC in the area.

By 1977 word was well and truly out, and many other conservationists began taking the trip down the Franklin. Images, which became so vital in the campaign to save the river, also started spilling out into the national media, including Peter Dombrovskis' famous image of Rock Island Bend on the lower Franklin.

Dombrovskis was born of Latvian parents in Germany at the end of World War II and had come to Australia as a refugee in 1950. As revealed in the recent film documentary *Wildness*, Dombrovskis had been a wilderness photographer in Tasmania and early exponent of environmental conservation for many years prior to the Franklin campaign. Dombrovskis, along with wilderness photographer Olegas Truchanas (who had been Dombrovskis' mentor and one of the first photographers to bring the beauty of the Tasmanian wilderness to global attention) had previously documented Lake Pedder; narrating slide shows at Hobart Town Hall about the importance of preserving the beautiful Tasmanian environs they had photographed.

Tasmanian Wilderness Society meetings were moved to Hobart, and attracted swelling numbers of sympathisers. Brown recalls being shocked to hear a senior politician, Geoff Pearsall (then a senior Liberal opposition member of state parliament), use the word 'wilderness' to describe forests in one of the first TWS meetings in Hobart. It was a turning point, demonstrating that the language of conservation was slowly seeping through into the mainstream consciousness. Here was a conservative politician using the same terminology as conservationists, a group hitherto decried in the national mainstream as 'ratbag radicals'.

'I had never heard a senior figure in public ever use the word. It wasn't part of the spoken language except in the derogatory sense of the political wilderness or the biblical wilderness. An awful place . . . It hadn't become part of the public debate, I don't think, until the Pedder campaign, then the consequent Franklin campaign . . . It was a great breakthrough as far as I was concerned,' says Brown.

Conservation was suddenly on the agenda, but in Tasmania, the deep divisions were starting to spill out of the lounge rooms and into the streets. 'The line certainly wasn't clear-cut between those people who wanted the development and those who opposed it,' says Brown. 'Piners were a tough breed of people who'd worked enormously hard. In the end they were earning a living in the most extraordinarily difficult circumstances, but they were buoyed on by the environment that they had enjoyed at a time when the environment didn't mean what it means now.'

Brown's line, which he put at every opportunity during this build-up to the Franklin campaign, was a simple one. The river must be protected now in order that future generations may enjoy it, and moreover, the short-sighted politics of economic return must not be placed above the need to protect our natural environment. In Brown's view, it was a matter of, 'Whether they wanted their kith and kin—in other words the images of themselves, the likeness of themselves—further down the line to have this repository for enjoyment in all its spectrum of manifestations available for them. And beyond that again, for a smaller group of understanding people, the right of the river and its environs and its ecosystems to continue to exist as against a temporary destructive escapade by modern acquisitive materialist society.'

It is remarkable that such a direct and sincere message could become the fuse that ignited such deep divisions in Tasmania, and nationally.

❧ ❧ ❧

One of the arguments that Brown frequently had to fend off was that the environmentalists were being 'elitist'—that owing to the remoteness of the Franklin in Tasmania's south-west wilderness, only a small number of people actually get to enjoy it. His response to this criticism in the media was that we don't drive bulldozers or put jukeboxes in churches just to make them more accessible to the broad community; why should we treat nature differently? 'It's like saying that it's elitist to like Tchaikovsky or, for that matter, punk music simply because a small section of the public likes it and you don't understand it,' responded Brown.

'The argument about the rights of wilderness and the rights of . . . species of life other than ourselves—and remember, they're not separate; we're an expression of them and they're an expression of us—exists because it exists. The only way it can be seen as elite is that . . . those people who either don't understand it or who abhor it find the easiest form of tackling that argument is to call it elitist.'

Nonetheless, support started pouring in from unexpected quarters. Brown tells the story of one elderly piner who approached him in Launceston to make a symbolic gesture of support. Brown recalls the piner strolling down the street toward him in Launceston, with a singular certainty of purpose. He must have waited for the right moment to greet Brown, and his gesture was a simple and deeply symbolic one: he handed Brown a small piece of Huon pine.

'It wasn't worked [crafted], it was just a leftover bit, a little bit—and he offered his encouragement and support and thanked us for what we were doing. It was magnificent because so many people were hostile from the region and we copped it verbally very often, and this old guy had the fore-thought and the courage. [It] gave a very clear connection between the rivers he'd worked and the rivers we were fighting for. I could then take and show [the wood] to other people as a symbol of the support not only that he was personally giving us, but that a past breed of people like him would have been giving us if they'd been there in bigger numbers.'

'All my being on . . . guard was defeated by the amity and the friendliness and the support that this man had given. And off he went—never saw him again. That sort of support came all over the place around Tasmania, [and] elsewhere around Australia. We copped hostility as well quite gratuitously, sometimes in the most surprising places. He might not have known it, but he was handing across an enormous piece of empowerment to us in doing so,' says Brown.

By 1977, Brown had given up on the idea of working full time as a GP. He spent longer periods alone at Liffey, noting in his diaries from the time that he did suffer considerably from the isolation, but ever strengthening his resolve to do what he could to right the wrongs of modern industrialisation he witnessed taking place around him. 'I opted to take a risk with my life rather than live to regret it,' he told the *Age*. 'There are times when I feel lonely and wonder about the $100 000 I could be earning in practice. But I am also very aware that very few people really understand what they are facing in the world, just as few understand the implications of the dams issue.'

Brown's lobbying for improved local bikeways continued, as did his concerns regarding Australia's burgeoning nuclear ambitions. But, as history demonstrates, the Franklin campaign was about to draw him into the thick of high-profile national lobbying, and again reflect his symbiotic relationship with the evolution of Tasmania itself.

He returned to the river with Paul Smith to shoot the film they had pledged to produce following their first trip. The film was made, and Brown says it proved to be incredibly important as part of an overall national engagement with the wonder of the river. It was completed at a time when colour television was making its way into the homes of Australians of all classes, giving the Franklin campaigners a new and potent medium: they were able to speak directly to people in their lounge rooms across the country.

'It [the Franklin] certainly needed the advocates of the Wilderness Society and from elsewhere speaking in its defence. It needed the arguments about the future so-called development of heavy industry in particular in Tasmania, the projected power demands for the state, and a whole host of other political and social questions.' But at the end of the day, says Brown, it was an aesthetic question about the relationship of that river with the hearts of people who had come from wilderness themselves.

'I'm using the term aesthetic in a very wide sense there to mean the impact on the human heart, the value that it brings to human life, the expression of that bond with nature which is in all of us. And the Franklin dam, as with so many other similar disastrous schemes around the planet . . . [was] drawing us to question how much we ignored things that we couldn't put a dollar value to. That's what it is about,' he says.

In the most literal sense, Brown was fusing his own identity with that of the river. Smith and Brown had taken to giving names to certain areas of the river that had a particularly profound effect on them. Brown says he hoped that if these areas were given names that adequately reflected their natural wonder, the chances of saving the river might be improved. Brown wrote to the authority responsible for naming such environments, the Nomenclature Board, and many of his suggestions—including the renaming of Deception Gorge as the Great Ravine—were accepted. This was to become crucial later, when representatives of the HEC and the Tasmanian Government actively tried to promote the idea that the river was not, in fact, beautiful at all.

Brown took a helicopter flight over the area with, among others, the HEC commissioner Russell Ashton some years later. As they passed over Rock Island Bend, Ashton turned to those on board, pointed down and said, 'Look, it's not beautiful like they say in the pictures, is it? It's not beautiful at all!' Robin Gray, who was to become Tasmanian Premier in 1982, later described the Franklin as 'nothing but a brown, leech-ridden ditch'.

There was expert assistance on hand to move the campaign forward from the early days. Brown says the impact of people like ABC journalist Peter Thompson cannot be overstated; Thompson advised the Franklin activists on the best course of action to take in terms of getting the ear of the national media. Thompson also joined Brown and Smith on that second Franklin trip when the film was made, and added a vital political nous and media-savvy dimension to the campaign. 'Peter's role is crucial,' said Brown. 'The dam would be there if he hadn't been there.'

Thompson, for his part, says he was learning along with everyone else. 'For a number of years, we were critical in each other's development, as great friends and collaborators,' he says. 'My background was media, but I wasn't an expert. I was a sports reporter for a year, did a small current affairs program on commercial radio, and presented *This Day Tonight*. But all that time, I had been spending a lot of time with Bob, rafted the Franklin and decided that was something I wanted to put my energies toward. But I had no master plans about how you manipulate the media. I was interested in the media and felt comfortable with it. It was the element of the campaign I naturally immersed myself in. And it was obvious that the campaign was only going to be successful through the media. It was a monumentally big story in Tasmania.'

By September 1977, the Tasmanian Government's Cartland committee had released to state parliament their report regarding land management in south-west Tasmania. In it, they recommended that all 'existing rights' to mining, forestry or hydro-electrical development should go ahead.

The Cartland Report sent shock waves through the conservation movement, and brought about a perceived split within the TWS. Both Bob Brown and Dr Norm Sanders, a former TV presenter and the director of TWS at the time, issued press releases with a perceivable difference in tone. Brown's release attempted balance by welcoming the 'positive' aspects of the report, such as its acknowledgment that certain parts of Tasmania were World Heritage-listed. In contrast, Sanders' response had completely slammed every aspect of the Cartland committee's findings, regarding any softer response to be political pandering.

Sanders resigned over the incident, and Brown put his hand up as willing to stand for the position of TWS director. He was appointed unopposed. Despite the unfortunate circumstances around his elevation to the position, the deed was done, and Brown quickly embraced his new role at the helm of Tasmania's paramount environmental organisation. Sanders would emerge again in 1980, swept into the Tasmanian House of Assembly as a Democrat on a wave of anti-dam sentiment.

Brown appeared on Tasmanian television in his first lengthy

interview in late 1977 discussing TWS opposition to any moves to dam the Franklin, and expressing concern about the directives contained in the Cartland Report. The interview was a turning point for Brown in overcoming his fear of public speaking, although it had to be filmed several times owing to Brown's nervousness and stuttering. Bob Brown was still getting a feel for being a media spokesperson. He was on a steep learning curve; he had been thrust into the centre of a storm. Despite the initial botched attempts, he eventually managed to get his key messages across very effectively, and the interview went national.

Brown immediately distinguished himself as part of a new breed of environmentalists in his role of TWS director. He was all for open dialogue, and for spending up big in order to get results. He immediately lobbied for the support of the Australian Conservation Foundation, who had been notoriously impotent throughout the Lake Pedder campaign, in helping finance the rising Franklin campaign.

The truth was that the TWS needed all the support they could muster; HEC plans were already well under way. Bob Brown knew it better than anyone.

Thick Chapter 7
of the torrent

T
he Tasmanian Hydro-Electric Commission had development designs on the Franklin and Lower Gordon rivers
as early as 1916. But throughout the 1970s, the plans
had materialised into concrete steps toward establishing a
series of dams. The HEC had already spent over $6 million in
preparation and planning, and had drafted exhaustive environmental impact reports in anticipation of challenges from
environmentalists and local tourism operators. They must
have known they would have a tussle on their hands, particularly after the heated debate that Pedder had generated.

Deni Hamill remembers the extent of the division in Strahan
and the nearby west coast communities. 'We'd just come off the
Lake Pedder campaign,' he says of the time the Franklin issue
started hotting up. 'We were involved in the petition against
Lake Pedder—that created a lot of controversy, but it also
created a lot of awareness of what we were liable to lose here.'

In May 1978 the TWS produced its first publication outlining the importance of preserving the river, entitled *The*

Franklin: Tasmania's Last Wild River. Bob Brown wrote the introduction, and Helen Gee put the 28-page publication together at breakneck speed. The HEC responded with the 2000-page *Report on the Gordon River Power Development Stage Two*.

As the stakes around the Franklin issue continued to rise, and national media started paying attention, the demands on Bob intensified. He was spending more and more time at the Wilderness Society office in Hobart, and making the trip to and from Liffey every day became completely impractical. On many occasions he would sleep on the floor at friends' houses, pushed to the brink of total exhaustion. Having no income throughout the entire Franklin campaign, he very much had to rely on the generosity and support of other Franklin activists.

Within Tasmanian and national politics things were in a state of rapid flux. The longstanding conservative ALP leader Eric Reece, who had been one of the HEC's most outspoken defenders, had retired in 1975. After some reshuffling a fresh-faced young premier with a strong belief in consultative politics, Doug Lowe, was appointed as leader. Brown and Lowe developed a relationship of mutual respect after a number of meetings to discuss HEC plans.

The fact that Lowe had initiated such meetings was remarkable enough—Tasmania had very much been the domain of the untouchable political elite prior to that. Brown had a good feeling about Lowe—here was a man he could talk to. Even though Brown still retained fragments of his characteristic bumbling nature, he was getting plenty of confidence-building experience under his belt. Brown later said of Lowe: 'He has been portrayed as vacillating and criticised roundly, but he was a decent warm-hearted human being. And in a revolutionary move, he invited we conservationists in to talk with him as Premier once every three months for a morning.'

Brown was learning fast how to play the media. He had received an informal promise from the editor of the Launceston

Examiner, Michael Courtney: if a reputable opinion poll was produced proving the majority of Tasmanians opposed damming the Franklin, he would run it on the front page. By June 1979 such a poll was completed. Courtney kept his word, and the remarkable findings that 53.5 per cent of Tasmanians opposed the dam was published on page one.

It put wind into the sails of the Franklin campaign at a pivotal time. It was another sign that the mood of the public had altered, and TWS started to firmly believe they had a chance. There was optimism in the camp.

TWS was rapidly expanding, and by 1980 had a new larger office, a Wilderness Society shop in Hobart's central business district, and over 1000 paid-up members. Brown was busy organising international support for the campaign, making contacts in Europe and America whose endorsements were to become invaluable. Consumer advocate Ralph Nader paid a visit, adding an increasingly higher profile to the national media coverage. TWS had staged some of Hobart's biggest ever street demonstrations, attracting crowds of 10 000, had produced films, and garnered 40 000 signatures for the 'Save the River' petition. Crowds in Melbourne and Sydney 'Save the Franklin' rallies were also swelling to record numbers.

Brown accompanied a young film-maker, Michael Cordell, on another Franklin expedition to produce another film, which resulted in the documentary *Franklin: Wild River*. These films, along with footage from British botanist David Bellamy, were to become vital components in the identity of the Franklin in the national psyche.

Premier Lowe was equivocal. He offered Brown a compromise that he would save the Franklin, but a dam in the Gordon above Olga rivers would go ahead. Brown said this would be completely unacceptable to the TWS. The HEC had their own opinion poll produced, in which they put the question: 'The HEC has proposed that parliament should approve a hydro development scheme on the Lower Gordon as a means of supplying Tasmanian electricity after the year 1990. Are you in favour or not in favour of this proposal?' The result was 56 per cent in favour, 40 per cent against.

By the time the issue was due to be voted in the Tasmanian Parliament, Premier Lowe had changed his position—he now threw his support behind the dam. In the first ever occasion of a member of the public being invited to address the Tasmanian House of Assembly, Bob Brown was asked to give a short speech to the parliament regarding the Franklin. He did so in June 1980, in a ten-minute address, reminding parliamentarians of the extent of community opposition to the dam, and of their rare opportunity to protect this irreplaceable natural asset. 'I said that the Gordon below Franklin dam will bring the whole of this country down on your head,' recalls Brown.

Then, in a remarkable twist, Lowe changed his mind again. This time, it was a public display of emotion that seemed to have swayed him. The Premier was attending a launch of the feature film *Manganinnie*, the Tasmanian Film Corporation's first feature-length production. However, before it was shown, Bob Connolly's documentary *Franklin River Journey* was screened. The response in the auditorium was extraordinary.

At the end of the film there was a burst of sympathetic applause. But when this died down someone shouted 'Save the Franklin'. Immediately the entire audience rose to its feet and began a sustained and extraordinary burst of applause and cheering that lasted for some minutes. They were not applauding the film, they were applauding the river . . . The cream of Tasmanian society, from the Governor down, had filled the cinema and for the most part they were now on their feet, giving loud and lengthy vent to their feelings about the Franklin River . . . When the applause died down all eyes were on the premier. He sat white-faced, visibly moved by the spontaneous demonstration of feeling.

Lowe later recalled that moment. 'Many who have written on this subject since that day have portrayed that instant as my moment of decision,' Lowe later wrote. 'It was not. I had resolved within my own conscience my outstanding doubts on the Gordon above Olga Scheme much earlier in the day. I would be less than honest, however, if I did not say that I felt profoundly moved by the genuine feelings expressed by such a wide cross-section of notable Tasmanian people present that evening.'

He put his position to the next sitting of parliament that the Franklin must be saved. On Friday 11 July, 1980 he called a press conference to announce that the government had adopted its new position—no dam would be built on the Franklin. Despite an outburst of celebration within the TWS headquarters, there was lingering disappointment. Even though the Franklin was to be saved, it was to be at the expense of the next worst outcome—the Gordon above Olga dam would still be a destructive environmental blight on south-west Tasmania.

Then something remarkable happened, the two houses of the Tasmanian parliament split over the way to move forward. The Hare-Clark system in use in Tasmania's five House of Assembly electorates allowed each electorate to choose seven members by proportional representation. This voting method made it easier for small parties to gain parliamentary representation, reflecting their degree of support within the electorate. At the time of the dam debate, representatives only required 12 per cent of the vote to get elected. This has since been revised to require 17 per cent of the vote and only five members are now elected in each of the five House of Assembly electorates.

Thus the House of Assembly is often composed of independents, and had been a bastion of Tasmanian conservatism for years prior. The HEC had lobbied the Legislative Council, which employs a 'first past the post' (with or without preferences) voting system, intensely over the Franklin bill. The Legislative council unanimously voted to substitute the words 'Gordon below Franklin' in place of 'Gordon above Olga'.

Work on the Gordon below Franklin dam, should commence immediately. The bill was returned to the House of Assembly just before Christmas 1980.

'Without the Legislative Council causing that delay, there is again no doubt that [the] Gordon above Olga scheme would have been built, and it was very dicey indeed getting through that minefield,' said Brown.

With the parliament deadlocked in separate, although both unsatisfactory positions, Bob Brown knew that now was the time to expand the campaign as far afield as possible. Reporters from as far off as Paris newspaper *Le Monde*, the *Chicago Tribune*, the *Far East Economic Review*, a Helsinki newspaper, *Pravda*, *New Idea* and *Time* magazine ran articles on the Franklin—often quoting Bob Brown.

Despite the fact that the Melbourne *Age* newspaper eventually became one of the strongest advocates for saving the Franklin, Bob personally met the editor and received a lukewarm response.

'I'd been to see the editor of the *Age*, [and said]: "Look, we're having this blockade. It's going to be of enormous significance. We are not going to give up on this river". . . I went through the political background whereby the Fraser Government was in power but was not going to help us. There was the potential for a Labor government to come in and help us in the wake of the national Labor Party conference in Canberra that had decided so narrowly to go in favour of the No Dams policy. And he'd said, "Look, this is really not of interest to us". He took some convincing and he didn't give a commitment then that they would send somebody down. In the event, they certainly did.'

By 1980, the *Age* had adopted a strong anti-dam editorial position in regard to the Franklin, producing headlines such as 'The Franklin must be saved' in December of that year. 'The beauty of the wild, scenic rivers of south-west Tasmania has become known to millions of Australians in recent months through books and photographs.' The paper went on to state that damming the river would 'be a step backwards' into 'an ethos which regards no environmental treasure as safe from man ... The Premier, Mr Lowe, and his government should stand firm to save the Franklin. And the Federal government, which represents all Australians, should use its influence—and power of the purse—to ensure that the gorges of the Franklin are preserved as a national park for Australians, and the world, of the future.'

❧ ❧ ❧

The focus now was to garner as much federal political interest as possible. The support of the Australian Democrats and the ALP was galvanised when Don Chipp took a rafting trip down the Franklin with his wife in early 1981, and ALP environment spokesperson Stewart West established links with the Wilderness Society and met with Brown. West made it plain to TWS that the federal ALP was opposed to the dam.

Back in Hobart, despite hostility from the Legislative Council, Premier Lowe was pushing forward with his plan to establish the Wild Rivers National Park, locking away the Franklin, but continuing with plans to dam Gordon above Olga. He sought to have World Heritage status approved for the south-west Tasmania region. Lowe sought support from Canberra to proceed with this course of action, and had the full support of his inner Cabinet on 30 April 1981. Brown and Lowe met a week later, and reached an impasse—Brown would never give his approval to ripping into the heart of south-west Tasmania, whether it be through damming the Franklin or the Olga rivers.

Lowe wrote:

The development of this package was lauded by those who were seeking a genuine compromise on this issue of the

state's future power needs, but was vilified by those proponents of hydro-industrialisation who saw compromise as a
sign of weakness. It would also be insufficient to satisfy the
growing force of the Tasmanian Wilderness Society behind
its leader, Bob Brown.

Lowe was feeling the heat. The HEC organised a rally
outside Parliament House in Hobart in June 1981, and the
Premier narrowly survived a leadership challenge from pro-dam
Cabinet member Harry Holgate. The Holgate-led pro-dam camp
pushed for a referendum on the Franklin issue, and after
numerous Cabinet reshuffles, the Tasmanian ALP was in serious
danger of implosion. Lowe was losing his grip on leadership.

Meanwhile, Brown was being pushed to the edge of
exhaustion through the strain of managing TWS affairs and
retaining his focus squarely on the Franklin. It was to be a
time of great leadership skill-building for Brown, as Peter
Thompson recalls. 'He had a natural genius for leadership,'
says Thompson. 'There is an alignment about him.'

The fact that Bob Brown didn't have his own dependent
family was a factor that freed him up to lead the campaign.
Thompson says, 'The family that Bob Brown developed was
the Franklin family, now I suppose it's the Greens family'. The
fact that Brown had no direct income throughout the six years
of the Franklin campaign also benefited him in the eyes of
many of the young activists who enlisted. 'There was this
whole body of young, committed activists who were giving
tremendous amounts of their own time for nothing. That gave
him a tremendous liberation and connection. It suited his
asceticism—that he could live like that and still feel comfortable. He had been in material self-denial for years, and people
were finding that quite attractive, and I think quite a factor in
the powers of his developing authority and leadership,' says
Thompson.

Other factors that came into play were the fact that Brown
didn't have any intimate entanglements with anyone in the

campaign. But the most important leadership attribute Brown possessed was his fierce, passionate belief in the cause—the river must be saved.

'The development of his shining intelligence was in knowing he had to manage these relationships with the many people around him. There was no shortage of discord, and the potential for tension and running off the rails,' Thompson admits. The issues that often besiege voluntary collectively run organisations were rearing their head within TWS. Meetings were becoming long drawn-out affairs of endless quests for consensus, over often trivial matters. Accusations of sexism and abuse of hierarchy were aired. A consensus was reached on the need for TWS to move forward through the tenets of non-violent direct action.

'There developed a very strong feminist view that it was an outfit run by men with Bob Brown and myself at the top,' says Thompson. 'There was a perception that it was a closed decision-making group, run by Bob in particular. That was an immensely dangerous perception that could have destroyed the whole campaign. We were only just hanging in there as it was. The blockade gave more of an outlet for the earthy sense that everybody is involved in the process.'

'Bob would not always navigate those sorts of issues well,' says Thompson. 'He always worked to a point of personal exhaustion to keep the avenues of communication open. He did his utmost to be inclusive. He'd never see anyone within the TWS as the enemy camp. Like the emerging feminist group in the TWS, he would never think he had to defeat those people. Others in the TWS may have seen it in . . . battle metaphor terms. Bob realised that it had to be kept together. He would be constantly racking his brain about how it might be made better. TWS did move to a more consensus decision-making structure, but there were stress lines everywhere. I'm sure he still has these problems with the Greens.'

Brown was doing his best to move the campaign forward. He called on expert advice from overseas to suggest alternatives to the dam option for the south-west. He made contact with the Governor of California, Jerry Brown, requesting he send his expert on Energy and Communication, Deni Greene, who was to spend two weeks in Hobart. Bob says Greene's role was crucial in that the HEC dismissed TWS as a bunch of cranks, yet here was an expert saying more or less the same things. However, her gender created another problem for HEC representatives.

'She was an expert in cogeneration and energy efficiency and alternative energy usage,' says Brown. 'When she got a message—she was flying between San Francisco and Washington—that there'd been a request for her to go to Tasmania, she was completely nonplussed. It's an emormous credit to her that she did come.' Brown says when Greene fronted the HEC engineers 'they had sweat running down their faces'. 'They knew . . . how to deal with and talk to males. But the times were changing and here was a female engineer and they could not deal with it,' he said.

She met with the HEC on numerous occasions, and left TWS with the positive news that she had never seen a development swamped with such fierce opposition make it through to eventual completion.

Meanwhile, the referendum option was passed. At a press conference that evening, Lowe said the referendum would contain a 'No Dams' option. It was a tactical error, because the final referendum contained no such option. Lowe would later have to cave in to party pressure that to place a 'No Dams' option would be irresponsible for Tasmania's energy future, and the choice would therefore be between the Franklin or Olga dams. Lowe's leadership had been undermined, and his days were numbered.

The TWS secured a budget from ACF of $100 000 to run its referendum campaign. After lengthy discussion, and the employment of a professional advertising agency to assist with PR and test the electorate, TWS adopted the line that the best strategy would be to advocate for an informal vote to the

Canberra, 1969.

London, 1970.

At Liffey, 1974. PHOTO BY FRANCES NEWMAN.

In the Irenabyss (chasm) on the Franklin River, 1980.
PHOTO: LES O'ROURKE/FAIRFAX PHOTOS

Bob in his motorised Overcoat, Hobart, 1981. PHOTO BY AMANDA STARK.

With the actress Lorraine Bayly, Franklin River campaign, Hobart, 1981.

Ironing a shirt on the run.

Addressing a crowd in the Lemonthyme at the declaration
of the national park, 1983. PHOTO BY CHRISTINE MILNE.

Announcing that Tasmania Wilderness Society will support the Labor Party and the Democrats in the federal election, Melbourne, 1983. PHOTO BY ROSS SCOTT.

During the Daintree campaign, 1983. PHOTO BY SANDY SCHELTEMA.

With Bob Hawke (left) and Claudio Alcorso (right), federal election campaign, Hobart, 1983. Senior Labor figures Neal Blewett and Barry Jones are in the background.

With dad Jack and Judy Henderson, Liffey, 1985. PHOTO BY REX DIREEN.

With fellow campaigner and journalist Peter Thompson.
PHOTO BY TASMANIAN WILDERNESS SOCIETY.

Climbing down Cruach Ardrain, Scotland.

Bob as director of the Tasmanian Wilderness Society with Norm Sanders (right), at a protest rally in Franklin Square, Hobart, 1983. Australian Information Service
PHOTOGRAPHY BY JOHN MCKINNON.

referendum. Stewart West contacted TWS to advise that ALP had adopted a no-dams position federally.

In the meantime, the Tasmanian Liberals were moving into predator mode. They had replaced opposition leader Geoff Pearsall with Robin Gray, a pro-dams hardliner who sits on the board of directors of the Tasmanian timber company Gunns Limited today. Brown knew the appointment of Gray would stand the Liberals in strong stead to win the next state election, particularly with the ALP in such a divided state.

Harry Holgate had distributed a petition among ALP members calling on Lowe's resignation. It was successful. Lowe was out, not only as premier, but he elected to sever his membership with the ALP.

'When the House of Assembly resumed that afternoon, I took my seat on the crossbench next to the Australian Democrats member for Denison, Dr Norm Sanders,' wrote Lowe.

> It was a strange feeling and I suddenly realised that I was seated just four places along from where I had originally taken up my position in the House of Assembly four years earlier. During that time I had progressed through to the heights of government leadership and suddenly had found that the roller-coaster of political reality had brought me back virtually to the position from where my parliamentary career had begun.

It was the issue of the Franklin that had fuelled that roller-coaster, split the ALP, and was still far from resolved.

Federally, despite mounting pressure, Malcolm Fraser was unwilling to budge on the Franklin, declaring it a state issue. However, within the federal ALP, opposition was building. At the party's state conference in 1981, a majority of party delegates voted against building dams in the Gordon or Franklin River, meaning both the ALP and the Democrats would go to the next federal election on a no-dams platform. It was a promising sign, but it is always easier for a party in opposition to take a hardline stance. Would they be willing to hold their no-dams position at crunch time?

The referendum went ahead at the insistence of the new ALP Premier Harry Holgate in mid-December 1981. The HEC had the financial advantage of two to three times the budget of TWS to promote their case. TWS had the advantage of 1500 volunteers doorknocking households across the state advocating the 'vote informal' option—it was the kind of grassroots support the HEC could never match. A no-dams rally in Launceston one week before referendum day attracted close to 3000 people. TWS opponents 'may be vocal', said Brown, 'but they can't find that sort of support from people'. Bob Brown received a death threat prior to the rally, and later stated his concern that the gunman might have mistakenly hit someone else.

The final result was 47 per cent supporting the Gordon below Franklin dam, 8 per cent supporting the Olga option, and 45 per cent voting informal. It put the new Holgate ALP Government in dire straits. The same ALP government that had eighteen months before opposed flooding the Franklin was now supporting it again, albeit with a new premier.

Brown told Holgate that if the government proceeded with the dam, the crossbench (now made up of Democrat Norm Sanders, ex-ALP Lowe, and another ex-ALP member for Bass, Mary Willey, who had quit the party in disgust at Holgate's power grab), would force an election and the government would be crushed by Gray's conservative opposition. Mary Willey was later to say that she wanted to do something for the south-west, 'I've got this faith in Bob Brown, this tremendous belief,' she said. Gray already had the support of the diehard pro-dammers. Federal ALP spokesman Stewart West had a similar message to translate to Holgate when the pair met in Melbourne on 20 January 1982—that the Tasmanian ALP was on a suicide course.

By 24 January a new trump card arrived for the conservationists. The federal government announced that it had nominated Tasmania's south-west, including the Franklin, for World Heritage listing.

Meanwhile, the fireworks continued in the Tasmanian Parliament. At the first sitting for 1982 on 26 March, the Gray opposition supported a no-confidence motion passed by Norm Sanders against Holgate. An election was called—to be held on 15 May. Gray promised to begin work on the Gordon below Franklin dam as soon as humanly possible.

After much deliberation, Brown decided he would run for Tasmanian Parliament to join those on the crossbench. Brown said: 'I'm not a career politician, I'm not a politician in the conventional sense at all.' But he feared that the two major parties were conspiring to make the Franklin a non-issue, and that was why he would stand.

TWS surveying had indicated that he would stand the best chance in the seat of Denison. The Bob Brown smear campaign had been launched. It was deeply personal and hurtful, involving reprinting and letterboxing an *Examiner* article on his sexuality.

In the lead-up to the election, US warships *Truxton* and *Duncan* arrived in Hobart, and Brown felt a serious dilemma about whether to speak out so close to the election—feeling torn between the issues of saving the Franklin or opposing nuclear terror. He elected to speak.

Brown didn't get the numbers, although he was the highest vote-winner not elected. The result was a landslide victory to Gray. It certainly marked a grey day for the TWS. The last hope now rested on federal intervention. Brown soon after began a national tour, speaking at demonstrations all over the country calling for the federal government to intervene.

The Tasmanian Wilderness Society lost an attempted High Court case that sought to restrain the Commonwealth from giving loan funds to Tasmania to build the dam. It was taken in Tasmania as a national seal of approval. Meanwhile at the next ALP national conference in Canberra a team of TWS spokespeople, led by Brown, lobbied furiously. The result was better than expected. John Button put an unexpected motion that the ALP would flat-out oppose the construction of the dam. It was passed by a clear majority. Bob Hawke was among those in the affirmative.

In Tasmania, Gray took up his premiership and passed the Gordon below Franklin dam proposal as the first legislative measure. Wasting no time, the bulldozers moved in and work began on the dam in late July 1982.

In Tasmania's west, Bob Brown was now being viewed as public enemy number one by many. He was seen as a clear and present threat to the livelihood of those who saw the HEC as providing much-needed income and job security. In research undertaken by TWS on the attitude of pro-dammers, the over-riding sentiment was one of deep hostility. 'Give me $50 000 and a shotgun and I'll tell you what Bob Brown is,' one of the respondents declared.

Robin Gray had issued statements warning that anyone— including the federal government—who attempted to intervene at this stage, would have a 'massive fight on their hands'. Malcolm Fraser had, however, refused to drop the World Heritage listing.

After months of scouting and planning, of protest work-shops being held all over the country, the Franklin blockade began on 14 December 1982—which, by a happy twist of fate, was exactly the same day the Franklin was declared a World Heritage-listed site. It was one of a number of fortuitous events that would ultimately steer the campaign to victory. The World Heritage committee in Paris had expressly advised against going ahead with the dam.

The crowds of blockaders started pouring in from all over the country. An opinion poll published in the *Sydney Morning Herald* in October 1982 indicated that 75 per cent opposed the dam. Botanist David Bellamy had publicly spoken out against the dam, as had Prince Charles. It was now an issue of international significance. Fraser still refused to intervene.

Brown had met with Robin Gray in early December in a last-ditch attempt to change his mind. Instead, Gray would not give any assurances to Brown, stating that he may proceed with other dams in the south-west region in his term of office. 'I asked him to declare a moratorium for a three-month period over Christmas while he negotiated with the federal government, but he refused. The time for negotiation is fast dying,' said Brown at the time. 'It seems they are determined to send the bulldozers in and so we are now preparing for the real fight we have been working toward for three years.'

As is the case with many environmental protests and blockades, the urge to get involved is more than just a political calling. As the Franklin had come to be recognised as a national symbol of renewal, it took on spiritual dimensions for the individuals involved in the campaign. Not only were they engaged in acts of civil disobedience to save a river, they were themselves merging with that natural environment.

For many of the thousands of city kids that were drawn to the Franklin, as is the case today with forest or anti-nuclear protests, such gatherings offer participants a rare opportunity to live in nature, while simultaneously fighting for its protection. This is a vitally empowering, life-changing experience.

Reg Morrison decided to throw his support behind the blockade, loaning and operating the *J. Lee M*—which became known as the 'Greenie Express'—to take the hordes of protesters on the four-hour journey from Strahan to the protest camp on the edge of the Gordon river. Deni Hamill became skipper of the Greenie Express. It is an experience he will never forget.

'It was a natural thing that I got caught up with the blockade—I was hooked on the river anyway,' says Hamill. 'We were up in Queensland and Reg said, "Would you do the blockade?" We came back to Hobart and worked with the ABC for a week or so, talking to them about what I thought would happen when the police came in. Then I took the *J. Lee M* and ran the transport to the blockade.'

Why did he agree to do it? 'I would say Bob Brown's influence had a lot to do with it. Bob Brown has a habit of doing that to people . . . He doesn't deliberately manipulate people, but he's got a very infectious personality. How did I get involved? I blame Bob Brown,' says Hamill. 'No, seriously, it's more about what's up there on the river, and how it affects you—it's very powerful stuff.'

Writing in the *Bulletin* magazine (on 1 February 1983), Lenore Nicklin described the scene at the protesters' base camp:

> After 14 days of continuous rain, the greenies' camp on the Gordon river was a soggy mess. Mud oozed and squelched everywhere. Rain seeped into tents and jeans, wool trousers and sweaters beneath the ubiquitous japaras were all damp and soaking. Never mind the leeches (they're quite benign really—only want a bit of a feed) some greenies went bare-footed. Others put plastic bags over their socks before pulling their boots on and others converted green garbage bags into amazing, three-tiered leggings ... The Hobart greenies are different from the Terania Creek greenies—veterans of the New South Wales clash against timber fellers—in that they are not dominated by the alternative society people. There are doctors, lawyers, university professors, teachers, neatly dressed, fresh-faced young women from Turramurra and South Yarra and grannies from Queensland.

In Strahan, the deep divisions within the community were reaching breaking point. Deni Hamill says he 'copped it pretty severely' from some quarters. 'There's no question that the town was divided over the blockade, it was completely divided. I come from the biggest family in Strahan—there are twelve of us; eleven boys and one girl. Naturally I copped it from some people, yes.'

'What really hurt were all the people you thought were friends, but they stuck the dirt in. That hurt a bit, more so than people you didn't care about. They had the Tasmanian Government behind them. We didn't have the government's support. Fair's fair. They'd say—"Most of these people are from interstate on the dole". Maybe some of them were, but a lot of them weren't. The majority of people in the blockade were women. But these are the people that actually cared too. These are the people that sacrificed their freedom to fight for what's around them,' he says.

'During the blockade, dealing with these people from all different parts, and seeing their love for the forests and all that—I feel very proud and privileged to have ever met any of them.'

Many activists who were involved in the Franklin campaign describe Bob Brown's ability to bring calm and order to proceedings with his very presence, and somewhat daggy gestures. Franklin blockader Rodney Waterman recounts such an occasion: 'I remember one crucial TWS national meeting, all in a huge circle tensely debating a difficult issue. Bob arrived with a big brown paper bag of jelly beans and walked around the group handing them out to all—the tension began to subside and we all cheered up!'

But for Brown and other key protest leaders, the stress was immense. 'I think, looking back on it, I was running at the end of my line and, thank glory, we had such a bond between those of us in the Wilderness Society who'd been flat-tack on this campaign for some years, because we looked after [each other]. There were tears very often, great distress at Strahan and back in Hobart where people were doing the organising, controlling the money. They were under siege at times . . . and soft-natured Wilderness Society people fighting for this river suddenly had to become highly organised and very determined to keep this enormous number of people in check, to make sure that the focus was kept on the river, to make sure that violence didn't occur.'

'So, the bag of chocolates would arrive on somebody's desk or the card and funny pictures or the bunch of flowers, which was a human dimension in that campaign which was utterly important to us to be able to survive it all.'

By the evening of 14 December, with a bevy of print and electronic media on hand, 53 arrests were made. By 16 December, Brown was arrested and sent to Risdon Prison. He refused to sign the bail conditions that stipulated he was not to 'lurk, loiter or secrete in' the HEC's World Heritage-listed area. A steady stream of arrests would continue over the next months—culminating on 1 March, later declared 'Green Day', when 228 arrests were made.

By 23 December, Norm Sanders had resigned his position within the parliament, stating that he couldn't sit back while the parliament 'drift(s) off into this totalitarian government'. The Tasmanian system dictates that the position can be filled by the next highest vote winner. It opened up the opportunity for Brown, and gave him plenty to consider in Risdon Prison.

The Franklin campaign spilled out across national borders, and the demands on Brown intensified. He was named Australian of the Year by the *Australian* newspaper for 1982, and gave a speech about it off the back of the *J. Lee M.*

Deni Hamill recalls: 'He made this speech off the back of the boat. She was full of protesters, and all up the banks of the river. I was up at the wheel-house, and they called me down. I said to Bob, "Yeah, you'll get the top job next". He said, "Oh, come on. I don't think I'd want it." That's the sort of guy Bob Brown is.'

A few days later, Brown found himself among the protesters in Risdon Prison. The image of his arrest became famous, Brown smiling and holding out his hand to the arresting officer. He says he remembers the officer speaking into his radio that he 'had found No. 1'—the code name for Bob Brown. But, as Brown recalls it, the young officer was shaking from the discovery. Also, says Brown, the officer was in serious danger of falling in the river, and he feared for the officer's safety.

'I've fortunately lived with policemen and women all my life, and I was extending that hand to him not to be hand-cuffed but to give him an anchor against falling back into the river. I remember that very clearly . . . the smile was to try and settle any anxiety he might have that there was going to be a fight or a struggle or an escape . . . he was very pleasant, the policeman.' Bob recalls that some of the police were onside with the protesters, occasionally lifting their caps to reveal a 'no dams' sticker.

Having grown up in a policeman's family, Brown was not daunted by the prospect of prison, although he says, 'I was aware of the indignity that was involved in being sent to gaol and I was very, very aware that this was putting onto my parents, in particular . . . a very troublesome question for them'.

Brown says many of those in Risdon Prison at the time felt that pressure of putting trouble on the shoulders of innocent people back home. He recalled one young man who had cried all night in the cells as he felt he was disgracing his parents. He says almost none of the people arrested at the Franklin had been to gaol before. It became a self-appointed task to keep up the spirits of those who were in the gaol at that time.

The presence of the protesters also resulted in a pay rise for the warders. 'The government, threatened with a strike, had to give them a pay rise,' as Brown recalls it. 'Suddenly Robin Gray's government had to reverse its previous decision . . . because it couldn't have withstood a warders' strike on top of two or three hundred extra inmates.'

The protesters also became something of a hit among the other prisoners, who 'got a kick out of it'. Brown was called to the assistance of one of the regular prisoners who had attempted suicide by cutting his wrists. 'I knew he wasn't going to die,' says Brown. 'It was just a matter of fixing him up until the ambulance arrived.' Brown says the incident immediately raised his status within the prison.

Despite the poor communication that sometimes existed throughout the previous years between Bob Brown and his father, such as his father's opposition to Brown's Mount Wellington protest, Jack Brown took his son's side. Jack and

Marjorie had seen the reports coming in on television about the Franklin arrests, and Jack had declared, 'That is enough for me,' and written to Malcolm Fraser that he would never get his vote again. This was a tremendous leap from a man who had been a policeman all his life, who'd had to deal with Vietnam protesters despite internal misgivings—to place himself in support of his son's civil disobedience.

In an article from the *Australian* newspaper of 1 January, 1983, Bob Brown wrote in a letter from his prison cell that he was being made to feel like a trespasser in his own cathedral.

> For several years I have returned to it [the south-west] to watch the interplay of forests, rivers and sky by day and to listen to the animals stir at night when the stars are ablaze and the scintillating blue specks of glow-worms pierce the forest floors of blackness.
>
> I am not a conventionally religious man, but in the wilderness I have come closest to finding myself and knowing the universe and accepting God—by which I mean accepting all that I don't know. The wilderness is my best place on earth. It is at least as important to me as a place of refreshment, inspiration and fulfilment as is the house of worship to many other Australians.
>
> Now I have been made a trespasser in the Cathedral of my choice.

The story also quoted Bob's parents saying: 'He grew up in the bush and was kindly and considerate to other people. When Bob became active in attempting to save the Franklin River from destruction he and his companions gained the full support of his family.'

A few days later a visitor brought him the parliamentary papers required to fill Norm Sanders's vacated seat in parliament—he signed them, stating that he might only stay in the position until the battle for the river was won. He also signed the court's bail conditions, clearly stating that he was doing so under protest. He later said that he would be willing to break the bail conditions because the HEC's edict banning the media and the protesters from the work site ran 'across the line of decency and morality' embraced by western civilisation. He had spent nineteen days behind bars.

Brown recalls that in Strahan, pandemonium was breaking out. The public phone at the airport was out, the phone booth in town was out, all phone and fax lines to the Wilderness Society had been cut. The only bridge out of the protesters' camp had been blocked by a police car. The road between the protest camp and the town of Strahan had been closed.

The bulldozers were heading through Strahan, and every effort had been made to stop the protesters from getting the news out. Recalls Brown, 'We discovered that the Wilderness Society shop, which was separate from the information centre, had a phone at the back that was still working. Using that phone . . . I was able to alert the national media.'

The situation made Brown remember the fate of Max Price and Brenda Hean during the Pedder campaign. 'We'd had death threats throughout the Franklin campaign . . . it was a sobering thought when you went back to what happened to those two people.'

A week after his election, Bob Brown was bashed in Strahan car park. The *Sydney Morning Herald* reported that Brown had been walking down a small side street when four young men attacked, one wielding a tyre lever. He was repeatedly kicked and punched to the ground, but somehow managed to get hold of the weapon before the men fled. Brown said he believed the violence was partly encouraged by the tone of reports in the Tasmanian press at the time, including one that had run in the Hobart *Mercury* under the headline: 'Violence expected at tomorrow's rally'. The four men were given suspended sentences. Miraculously, it was the only incident of serious violence to mark the Franklin protests.

Meanwhile, Prime Minister Malcolm Fraser was talking of an early election. He came to Tasmania and made a trip over the Franklin. At a press conference at Hobart airport he pledged that the federal government would give Tasmania $500 million to build a thermal power station instead of damming the Franklin. The offer was refused even as it was put. Fraser later admitted he knew it would be refused, but that he had attempted to inform the public of the federal government's position.

By 3 February, Fraser had announced his plans for a double-dissolution election, and Bill Hayden had resigned the federal ALP party leadership, meaning the contest was to be between Fraser and Hawke.

The ALP assured TWS that Hawke would maintain the no-dams line into the election. The next day Hobart was the scene of Australia's biggest-ever conservation rally, with up to 20 000 people taking to the streets to save the Franklin. Brown addressed the rally, and telegrams of support from all over the world were read to the crowd, including one from comedian Spike Milligan. HEC Commissioner Russell Ashton went public on 5 February in the *National Times* stating his farcical paranoia about the TWS: 'I believe some of their funds come from Eastern Bloc countries—but I have no way of proving that.'

The TWS, and the anti-dam protesters taking to the streets all over the country wouldn't have too long to wait.

By the beginning of March the ALP were victorious and Hawke stated in his victory speech that, 'The dam will not be built'. By 31 March the Hawke Government had passed regulations under the Australian National Parks and Wildlife Act forbidding further construction of the dam. Premier Gray announced the next day that the ruling would be ignored, that he had an electoral mandate to proceed with the dam, and that a challenge would be launched in the High Court. Hawke threatened to fine anyone working on the site $5000 if they proceeded. The High Court hearing would begin on 31 May.

Brown was now moving between Tasmania and the mainland, generating as much national pressure as possible to ensure Hawke held to his word. At a Melbourne Labour Day rally he informed crowds that work on the dam had been deliberately stepped up since Hawke had taken his anti-dam position. 'The HEC have gone flat-out to increase their work-force at the dam site in order to increase the rate of destruction.' Bulldozers, heavy machinery and chainsaws were 'dragging down the rainforest' in a frantic effort by the HEC and the state government to force the federal government to back down in the face of extensive damage to the World Heritage area, he said.

An officer of the Commonwealth Police warned Brown that Wilderness Society phones were being tapped. They said they would accept no calls from the Wilderness Society for that reason.

By the official end of the campaign on 8 March 1983, 4000 people had taken part and more than 1400 protesters had been arrested in the cause of river protection. TWS said it was no longer necessary to maintain the blockade, following assurances from Hawke that the dam would not go ahead.

❧ ❧ ❧

The High Court decision came on 1 July 1983. It was a 4:3 majority—the Franklin would be saved. The highest court in the land ruled that the newly elected Hawke Government's legislation to protect the area's World Heritage values, in line with Australia's obligations to the World Heritage Convention, overrode the Tasmanian Government's legislation to build the dam.

An editorial in Australia's strongest anti-dam newspaper, the *Age* on 4 July made the paper's position plain:

This newspaper campaigned against the construction of the Gordon below Franklin scheme on the grounds that the proposal by Tasmania's Hydro-Electric Commission to flood an area of rare beauty would constitute an attack against the environment that future generations of Australians would find difficult to understand. Naturally, we are pleased with the High Court judgement which now ensures that the section of Tasmania's south-west covered by the World Heritage listing will be preserved for posterity. The efforts of the environmentalists have been repaid. They fought a spirited and, at times, unconventional campaign which ended up in the highest court of the land.

At the midday Brisbane press conference after the court case, describing the decision as 'a people's victory', Brown set out his personal philosophy of optimism in the face of the inevitable tragedy of humankind's future.

> . . . hope comes from the fact that the community made this change. [We have acknowledged] that there is a limit to the technological destruction we can allow in the name of progress . . . I know that hope will go out from the decision to the people in the world who are fighting bigger issues, such as the nuclear arsenals that are aimed against the future of humanity, the imbalances between rich and poor . . .
>
> We have got some very big problems confronting us and let us not make any mistake about it, human history in the future is fraught with tragedy . . . It's only through people making a stand against that tragedy and being doggedly optimistic that we are going to win through. If you look at the plight of the human race it could well tip you into despair, so you have to be very strong.
>
> We all have to because we are bearing up against a world political community and military community that runs on ego. The people involved in this campaign by and large run on an ideal—the hope for a better human future—and it is not easy going all the time.

It was the voice of an idealist who had tasted victory, and his words touched the nation. Brown says it was appropriate at that moment of Franklin victory to translate that optimism to the many other environmental fights that were going on around the globe at the time, and that continue to this day.

Reflecting on the campaign's frenetic turn of events throughout which he had been thrust into the eye of the storm, Brown explains that he really had no idea what he was getting himself into after the rafting trip with Paul Smith. 'I can say this for myself, I never really sat down and thought—is this going to be easy or is this going to be hard? We just campaigned to save the river. And the ante kept being raised on both sides; we were busy thinking how best to make sure we weren't knocked out by it.'

'In that early period it was relaxed, because there were years to come, and it was a case of documenting the beauty of the river and getting people to know about it. I guess we felt naïvely, not having any inkling of the forces that could and would line up against us right across the spectrum, that if people got to see the beauty of this place then it wouldn't be flooded. It was pretty naïve . . . with the experience of Lake Pedder.'

Brown told the *Age* in March 1983 that once the battle for the Franklin was won, he planned to write a book on 'The Human Tragedy'. 'The human race has the technological resources to create terrible tragedies,' he said. 'The fight to stop the dam has, in a way, been a fight not only to preserve a beautiful wilderness area, but a fight against technological overkill.'

Beyond Chapter 8
the Franklin

Brown says it was prodding from United Tasmania Group founder Richard Jones that tipped the balance for him in favour of remaining in politics after the Franklin victory. Given the opportunity through the previous election recount after Norm Sanders quit the parliament (largely in disgust over the way the Franklin protesters were being treated) Brown took his opportunity to infiltrate the hallowed halls of the Tasmanian House of Legislative Assembly in January 1983.

Needless to say, he faced a hostile Tasmanian parliament, although he drew some moral support from former premier Doug Lowe. Brown and Lowe now sat together in the House of Assembly on the crossbench. Clearly, Brown had raised much ire in the Tasmanian Government over the previous years. He was now a world-renowned environmental defender, and here he was—a rat among the ranks of the people he had directly and publicly undermined—the Gray Liberal Government.

'It was tough going,' says Brown of the period. It sounds like a massive understatement. 'I was copping a fairly continuous serve from the Liberals in particular, but the ALP as well.' He repeatedly put motions that went without a seconder and lapsed. He announced his homosexuality in his maiden speech to the Tasmanian Parliament. He later tried to introduce gay law reform, and failed to get a seconder. Tasmania would have to wait for more than another decade before it was ready for that one to pass the parliament.

The Franklin issue continued to dominate parliament for the first six months Brown was a member, between January and July 1983, when the High Court ruling was made. Gray persisted with his line that work must continue on the dam, right up until the day the High Court made its ruling.

Bob Brown had exposed a raw nerve in Tasmanian society—the Hydro-Electric issue went right to the core of it. Launceston was the first city in the Southern Hemisphere to 'switch on' to a new hydro-electric power grid in 1895. There were many whose hatred of Brown would persist, as he seemed to personify peoples' fears that the world they had known—job security in development industries—might be coming to a grinding halt. There were many others whose deep respect for Brown would ensure his place in the Tasmanian Parliament for the next decade.

Brown's election had far-reaching implications for politics in Tasmania—and elsewhere. Although he was known and respected as a conservationist, he was carrying on the tradition that had been set in motion by Richard Jones in 1972 with the United Tasmania Group. That party had put forward a vision that went beyond environmentalism into the territory of participatory democracy, government accountability to the community, and fostering broad social policies for change. In order to achieve those ends, the early Tasmanian conservationists knew they would have to create a whole new political narrative—it simply wasn't going to happen within the closed, industry-pandering world of the state parliament.

Bob Brown was the first direct conduit of this vision in the parliament, but in time, many more would follow.

Meanwhile, Brown had his own personal issues to deal with, while simultaneously learning the ropes in the Tasmanian Parliament. His mother Marjorie had been getting increasingly ill with cancer over the course of the previous years. She now joined Bob at Liffey in the last days of her life. Brown says that throughout the entire Franklin campaign his mother had been a tremendous pillar of support. She had covertly sent him a $20 bill from her pension payments in an envelope with a letter of support and news from home every week.

On one occasion during the hectic first six months of 1983 when the fate of the Franklin was still uncertain, as Bob was on a whistlestop media tour through Armidale airport, he had phoned his parents to arrange a short rendezvous. He sat with his father Jack and obviously very ill mother for not more than twenty minutes, until he had to board the next plane. He recalls his mother's tears as he walked off to catch the plane, and his feeling deeply torn between family and activist commitments. He says the bond between him and his mother had been tremendously strengthening throughout the entire campaign.

In the week after the Franklin High Court decision was handed down in Brisbane, Brown went to visit his parents. Doctors had confirmed the news that Bob had suspected—his mother's cancer was obstructing her bowel, and it was clear that she didn't have long to live. It was only later at Liffey, as he sat with his mother on the grasslands immediately adjacent to his house, that Bob admitted he had known she was close to death but had kept it from her. He wanted to encourage her to at least retain the strength to come to Liffey and spend some time with him before the end.

Brown made the journey from Sydney back to Liffey with his mother, and recalls that his neighbours had set up the house in anticipation of their arrival. 'When I arrived back here with my mother the fuel stove had been placed in the kitchen and it was on and burning, the house was warm, there was a lace tablecloth with goods on the table, the whole place was set up by those neighbours.'

Bob Brown and his mother had several months together at Liffey, providing the opportunity to reflect together about the Franklin campaign, about how she viewed her coming death and about life itself. '. . . All those things, it's important you can talk with a person about and . . . you're lucky to be able to talk with a person who's dying, who's so close to you, about, which in our culture or through circumstances so often is robbed from people.'

Brown was travelling to and from parliament throughout this period, with his father also staying at the house, and the rest of the family coming and going intermittently. He still keeps a photograph of his mother in his kitchen, taken in 1981. In it, she is standing on the front porch of the Liffey house with daffodils in full springtime bloom in the background. He promised his mother before she died that he would always keep a photograph of her pinned up in the house for as long as he lived there.

'That was a terrific struggle for her to get down here. Just getting along the walkways at the airport in Sydney was a terrible effort for her, but she got here and for a little while she—relatively speaking—prospered until the inevitable came and she went downhill and quickly died.'

It wouldn't be too long before he was also nursing his father. Having suffered several heart attacks, Jack Brown's health was also quite precarious. Bob and Jack had a new friendship grow out of their relationship during the Franklin campaign, a time when Jack had developed a new-found respect for his son's outspoken political convictions. Throughout the next years, Jack would frequently come for lengthy stays at Liffey until his death in Hobart in 1989.

More that just facing a hostile Tasmanian Parliament in those first years of his parliamentary career after January

1983, Brown says he faced a parliament that simply 'didn't care', displaying indifference and open ridicule to this wayward doctor from Liffey. His parents might have at least been pleased that their son now had a solid income. It was the first time in years that this had been the case—he had survived throughout the Franklin campaign largely on the generosity and support of friends.

Making the Tasmanian Parliament home, Brown exercised his own variety of daggy sedition. He was said to wander around the less-frequented rooms and vaults switching off the lights that seemed to be perpetually left on. Some MPs took to placing sticky tape over the switches; Brown simply peeled the tape off again and made sure the lights remained off when they weren't needed.

Immediately after the Franklin decision came through in July, the Gray Government approved another two dams—the King and Henty/Anthony Schemes. Brown was the only member of the house opposing the dams. They both went ahead without proper environmental or economic impact studies. Brown says he suspects the national media, not to mention the TWS, were utterly exhausted after the Franklin campaign. The Hawke Government funded the new Tasmanian dam proposals, eager to re-establish a workable relationship with the state government.

The HEC were in full throttle forward momentum, nothing would slow them down. They were offered a $70 000 grant by the National Energy Commission (NERDEC) to investigate wind power potential in Tasmania. The offer was refused, despite merely being an offer for research money, with no strings attached.

From its humble beginnings of those sixteen activists at Brown's Liffey house, the TWS was now a large and respected environmental organisation with a budget of over $1 million per annum. Over the next decade it would fight numerous national campaigns, mainly over forest issues. But following being elected to power in part on the strength of its stand on the Franklin issue, federally the ALP would retain its environ-mental sympathies, particularly after Graham Richardson was given the Environment portfolio in 1987. Brown quit his position as director of the Tasmanian Wilderness Society in 1984.

❧ ❧ ❧

By the beginning of 1985, Bob was spending more time in Hobart than at Liffey. He moved in with his old schoolfriend Judy Henderson, into a house in Waterworks Road. Hender-son says Bob made a wonderful housemate, sharing her desire for a quiet, disciplined life. 'He's very easy to get along with,' says Henderson, 'although he gets cranky sometimes, like anyone'.

She says the amount of pressure from the outset on Brown as the only Green in the parliament, and attempting to cover the whole green constituency's agenda, was extraordinary. 'Tasmania was, and remains, a deeply divided society,' she says. 'From Pedder and the whole Franklin dam stopping— Bob was never forgiven for that by some people. He was the personification of the halting of development. A lot of that anger was focused on him personally.'

Brown says that his time as an independent in the Tas-manian Parliament throughout the 1980s was largely taken up in presenting issues that were identified as important by community groups and that would otherwise never have had an airing in the parliament, and were repeatedly knocked down. He remembers his first day, being introduced to the parliament by Doug Lowe and Andrew Lohrey, and 'trembling from head to toe'. He took the affirmation to Queen option, rather than to God.

'But the job had to be done,' says Brown, 'and I had the support from the Wilderness Society and other people outside.

I was also free then to mix it with other community groups who were involved in social justice questions, in women's issues, Aboriginal issues, gay issues. From that point of view there was enjoyment in being able to represent points of view of community groups who had been otherwise locked out of the political input system. This was much more in tune with the wider green philosophy which I'd always had, and a relief in its own way from the extraordinary focus of the wilderness battles that had preceded my getting into parliament.'

Some of the issues were conservation focused, such as opposing the logging of the Lemonthyme and southern forests, inappropriate development of the Frankland and Cradle ranges, and opposing the Wesley Vale pulp mill. Others were broader social issues introduced as private member's bills—freedom of information, death with dignity, lowering parliamentary salaries, gay law reform, banning the battery-hen industry and advocating a nuclear-free Tasmania. His 1987 bill to ban semi-automatic guns was howled down by both Liberal and Labor members of the House of Assembly.

Brown used his new status as leader of the successful Franklin campaign and Tasmanian MP to attempt to apply pressure nationally over a number of issues. In 1984 he lobbied Prime Minister Hawke to refuse the French ship, *Polarbjorn*, entry to Australian ports. Brown also generated national media over the French government's poisoning of Adélie penguin eggs to halt breeding while an airstrip was built at the French Antarctic base.

The following year he was in the national media again, this time deriding the Gray Government's plans to allow blue ribbon tourist developments in the Cradle Mountain National Park. Describing the plans as 'sponsored madness', Brown told the now defunct Melbourne *Herald* in July 1985 that, 'If people are in the Cradle Mountain National Park because they think they can rely on the huts, they should not be in the park. It's not a ramble, it is a walk for which one needs to be greatly prepared and well motivated.' He said the huts would create greater risks to bushwalkers in extreme conditions, being a dangerous mirage to normal bushwalkers and creating the situation where tour operators would have to turn people away even if they were trapped in blizzards. 'The worry is that we will continue to see this kind of creeping urbanisation, bordering on ribbon development, in our wilderness areas.'

Later that year the federal government came under further attack from Brown, when it renewed national woodchip export licences for the next fifteen years. It was a crucial move that saw federal legitimisation of the controversial practice of woodchipping. It was to set the agenda for environmental battles that would take place around Australia for the next twenty years.

Brown described the decision as 'one of the worst in Australia's history'.

'We will raise a huge campaign to save Australia's forests from Daintree to Tasmania, from Eden to Albany . . . The mood of the Franklin campaign has been totally erased by this decision,' he told the *Age* in December 1985. And in February 1986 he declared that, 'Australia's forests are already being overcut and cannot stand the impact of this voracious, wasteful industry'.

In 1986 a new Tasmanian Green, Dr Gerry Bates, was elected in the seat of Franklin to join Brown in the Tasmanian House of Assembly. Brown says the media were still unconvinced that the Greens posed a serious threat, or even constituted a significant presence in Tasmania. They were still considered to be a 'flash-in-the-pan' phenomenon that had arisen purely out of the Franklin spectacle, and would pass just as quickly into obscurity along with their champion Bob Brown. There remained what Brown describes as an 'old boys' network' dictating political debate in the state, 'which interconnects the corporate sector with the leading politicians of the day, and quite nicely the senior people involved in the media outlets'.

National development industries, including mining, forestry and power, were pouring huge amounts of resources into creating lobbying organisations throughout the 1980s, fearful that the Franklin could shift the template of environmental battles in the wrong direction for years to come. The National Association of Forest Industries was formed, and the Australian Mining Industry Council was established. These groups, which Brown has referred to as 'the forces of darkness', would pose formidable challenges to the agenda Brown was championing both in Tasmania and nationally, and lead to a period of stagnation for the conservation movement in Australia throughout the 1990s.

By 1986 Brown had another election campaign on his hands. In his characteristically unorthodox fashion, he went to the election stating that 'he'd like to be made redundant'. The comment in February 1986 formed a headline in the *Australian* newspaper which also quoted Brown talking about his dream that the major parties would take up the conservationists' calling and he could then 'return to the community'. No doubt national media also wished the Greens would disappear, as the Green independents popularity rose in Tasmania, so too did the warnings from the conservative press.

'The best thing that can happen is for us to be wiped out at the next election because one or other of the major parties has taken up our policies,' said Brown. 'I hope my future is not in politics.' Despite his reluctance, Brown was returned to office with 15.5 per cent of the vote in his seat of Denison in the 1986 state election. Bob Brown and Robin Gray were now considered to be the most influential politicians in Tasmania. They dominated the political stage, and it is hard to imagine two men whose world views could be further apart. It is also hard to imagine a more telling demonstration of the polarisation that now existed within Tasmania.

❦ ❦ ❦

Brown's education in the ways of politics was advancing apace. Two of the most significant environmental battles that took place in Tasmania throughout the 1980s were the battle for the forests of Farmhouse Creek, and opposition to the Wesley Vale pulp mill. Brown would end up getting shot at and manhandled by construction workers at Farmhouse Creek in March 1986.

Farmhouse Creek was a little-known stream in southern Tasmania, just outside the World Heritage area nominated by the Fraser Government in 1980. It covers an area of roughly 12.5 kilometres, a corridor of wilderness between the South-West National Park and the Hartz Mountains. The Gray Government was determined to move forward with plans to use its forests for woodchipping.

Conservationists set up a blockade on the road into the logging site at Farmhouse Creek, and on 7 March, 1986, Brown ended up with cuts and bruising after being dragged from under heavy construction equipment by members of the Forest Employment Action Group (FEAG). FEAG members later dismantled the protesters' blockade camp, where the conservationists had been camping for a fortnight prior. Fellow Green independent Gerry Bates told the *Age* that the police had stood by and watched as a group of forester vigilantes manhandled and assaulted protesters. On 9 March, when Brown attempted to return to the protest camp, five shots were fired in his direction from a van as he walked along the muddy track toward the campsite.

Tasmanian Forests minister Mr Groom had implemented trespass laws drafted during the Franklin protests, prohibiting entry to the Farmhouse Creek area without permits, obtainable only to forestry workers, police and the media. 'Anti-greenie' sentiment was strong in the nearby town of Geeveston, where some residents had begun displaying stickers with slogans such as 'Fertilise the forests. Doze in a Greenie'. The chairman of the FEAG, Mr Tony Armstrong, had agreed to meet with Brown to discuss the impasse, but by 13 March had changed his mind; there would be no consultation with the conservationists.

The Forest Industry Association of Tasmania (FIAT) then launched a national media campaign under the headline 'Reject the Bob Brown fiction about Farmhouse Creek'. In it FIAT quoted Brown's claims that 'Tasmanians will see bulldozers run to the top of the Western Tiers' and 'chainsaws on the fringes of Federation Peak'. The claims were then countered by reassurances that 'Timber harvesting will reach nowhere near the top of Western Tiers' and 'there will be at least 14 km of rugged South-West country, which will be fully protected, between the closest timber harvesting and Federation Peak'. The advertisement concluded by saying: 'Don't be hoodwinked by Bob Brown's fiction'.

In that same week, United Tasmania Group founder Richard Jones fell off a ladder in Hobart and struck his head. His injuries were fatal. The accident sent shock waves through the entire conservation movement. Jones was by then the director of Environmental Studies at the University of Tasmania and a life member of the Australian Conservation Foundation. Brown said to a Melbourne *Herald* reporter: 'It was people like Richard Jones and many, many others who created an awareness and an appreciation among people of [the environment]. Not me.' More than any other single figure, Jones had been a monumentally important inspiration for Brown. His loss was felt with dismay and sorrow.

By this time, Brown was moving between his role as state parliamentarian and frontline forest demonstrator. Meanwhile at Farmhouse Creek, there were conflicting claims about whether the site fell under the legal protection of the state. It lay within a National Estate area, and in 1980 was listed by the federal government as an area deemed to be part of Australia's national heritage. But the fact that it was just outside the nominated South-West World Heritage Area ultimately became its undoing. It became a symbol of the Gray Government's commitment to move forward with a strong logging industry in Tasmania, and a litmus test to prove that the Tasmanian Government was able to act without being gagged federally. After the protesters' camp was dismantled, under the protection of state police logging went ahead at Farmhouse Creek in May.

As the re-elected Green independents in the House of Assembly, Brown and Bates were horrified at the direction the Gray Government was taking. They declared that rather than standing down, as Brown had intimated in the lead-up to the election, they would seek to form an alliance of Green independents across the state.

'The time has come to realise that the Labor opposition is not an opposition,' said Brown to the *Australian* in December 1986. 'The parties are involved in a rush for the high middle ground in Tasmania, with a preoccupation with economic issues.'

With the Greens polling at around 17 per cent across the state in Tasmania by late 1986, they now took pole position of recording the highest Green vote in the world, with the next highest polling Green party being the rising West German Greens, at that time polling around 9 per cent.

The next battle to propel Tasmania into the national spotlight was over the Wesley Vale pulp mill, on Tasmania's north coast. Local schoolteacher, housewife and mother of two from Ulverstone, Christine Milne, who had been involved in the Franklin blockade, formed a broad alliance under the banner CROPS (Concerned Residents Opposed to Pulp mill Siting). 'After the Franklin I went back to teaching and got involved in the forest campaign throughout the '80s. Then they announced plans for the Wesley Vale pulp mill, which is in the district I come from,' she said.

North Broken Hill Limited, in partnership with Canadian mining and logging consortium Noranda, had announced plans for the 'world class' pulp mill by 1987. It would again polarise Tasmania, attract national media attention, and eventually be settled only through a state election. The protest campaign was significant in that it drew together such a diverse umbrella group of opponents—graziers, farmers, fishermen, and schoolteachers—all rallying against offshore multinational interests.

'With Wesley Vale the parameters of the environmental debate widened beyond wilderness and forest protection to touch on aspects of everyday life,' wrote Milne in *The Rest of the World is Watching*.

> The environment became mainstream, daily and all-pervasive . . . Wesley Vale was no 'single issue' but demonstrated the interconnectedness of environmental concern. Encompassed in the debate were: loss of native forests; appropriate land use; toxic pollution of air and waterways; depletion of greenhouse gases; contamination of food; recycling and waste; public health; community involvement in decision making; and local self-determination.

Milne says that Wesley Vale, because it was planned to be built on rich farming land and would pump toxic organochlorine into Bass Strait as well as excreting carcinogenic dioxins into the air, mobilised opposition from consumers across the board via their hip pockets. 'People were quick to respond to the message that to put chlorine-bleached products into the trolley was to say yes to pollution,' she wrote. Consumers and Wesley Vale locals took the campaign on board, the Gray Government threw its support behind the multinationals, announcing on North Broken Hill letterhead that parliament would be recalled in order for the legislation approving Wesley Vale to be passed.

To many observers, this bespoke the depths to which Tasmanian parliament had plummeted. Noted Tasmanian author Richard Flanagan wrote:

> . . . there was a strong sense that parliamentary politics had become divorced from the problems that people were now facing. The Tasmanian parliament has never been a significant force in Tasmanian politics . . . The business of

government has traditionally been done in near-total secrecy, away from parliament, to which only lip service is paid. From the 1970s the decline of the Tasmanian parliament became spectacular, its growing irrelevance demonstrated and exacerbated by the contempt for Westminster forms displayed by parliamentarians themselves, public bodies such as HEC, and companies such as North Broken Hill . . . A disdain best illustrated by the press release made by the Gray government in 1989, which announced the recall of parliament on North Broken Hill letterhead.

Brown had joined with Christine Milne in publicly denouncing the Wesley Vale plans, and went on a national tour outlining his opposition. In November 1988 he told a group of 400 people at Box Hill High School in Melbourne's south-east that if the mill in Tasmania went ahead, it would be followed by a similar development in Gippsland, then in New South Wales. Again, the Tasmanian activists were successful in garnering national media and federal political sympathy.

By February 1989 Hobart streets were again choked with crowds close to 10 000 opposing the Wesley Vale development. 'This is an absolute milestone,' said Brown in the *Age*. 'The whole Tasmanian community has been galvanised . . .'

Federally, Graham Richardson had expressed his displeasure at the lack of a proper environmental impact study (EIS) being put forward in regard to the project. When the federal government asked for a serious EIS, Noranda, the Canadian multinational company pursuing the development, withdrew its support, fearing such demands might be placed on the company in regard to its major projects in Canada. The whole Wesley Vale project came undone.

Brown continued to forge a strong relationship with the ALP federally, drawing on some of the momentum of the Franklin victory. 'We were lobbying strongly in Canberra on a wide front and issues like Daintree and Kakadu and the

Tasmanian forests were very important,' he says. 'Bob Hawke recognised this and made the point through not only going to the Daintree but in launching the campaign and handing the Global 500 awards across to Margaret Robertson and Joe Glascott and myself and making a statement about the Daintree at The Lodge.'

Brown says that the appointment of Graham Richardson into the federal Environment portfolio in 1986 ushered in a whole new era. 'It was a completely new era because Graham Richardson was in such a formidable position to get the triumvirate . . . of Hawke, Richardson and Keating to vote for the environmental issues of the day and they would always take Cabinet with them.'

Richardson was later to write in his autobiography *Whatever it Takes* how he became a Bob Brown convert:

> We walked around some of the area, sat by the lake and talked. Bob Brown wanted chunks of forest, or preferably the whole area, put into World Heritage classification and protected forever. So utterly convinced of his cause, Bob can be utterly convincing; his passion and sincerity are very difficult to overcome and by the time we arrived back in Hobart I was a convert. Having been shown the awesome forests and streams he wanted protected, I wanted to become a warrior for his cause. This was a bad day for the logging industry in Australia but a very good one for me, the environment movement and the Labor Party. It didn't take too long to work out that we had a perfect convergence: what was right was also popular.

Federal ALP narrowly won a second term of office in 1987, winning government on preferences made up of Democrat and Green votes. The Democrats were steadily increasing their national appeal throughout the 1980s, and Brown occasionally travelled to the mainland to lobby on the Democrats' behalf. 'The independent Greens in Western Australia and

Tasmania and the Democrats right around the country are the places to vote,' he said to the *Age* in 1990. 'People should vote green, green, green.'

On the home front, Bob had his own personal traumas to deal with. His father Jack had been in an uncertain state of health for many years, having suffered a number of heart attacks. By 1989 he had been diagnosed with serious skin cancer, with Bob, and Judy Henderson nursing him at their home in Waterworks Road, together with Janice, Ben and George who took it in turns to visit from the mainland.

But it got to the stage where Bob knew Jack would be better off in the hands of professional care. After several sessions of radiotherapy, Jack Brown eventually died in Bob's bedroom at Waterworks Road in 1989.

Meanwhile, the environmental lobby was now considered to be one of the strongest pressure groups in the country. The Democrats had doubled their national vote between 1987 and 1990.

Sensing rising support for the Greens, Premier Gray delayed the state elections until May 1989. The timing couldn't have been better for Brown and Gerry Bates, then still in the parliament as independents. Entering the election, the Gray Government had a three-seat majority of nineteen seats. The ALP held fourteen and the independents two.

Brown led a strong campaign, declaring that the Green independents stood for more than just the environment, but 'are also concerned with all issues that affect the community . . . The mainstream politicians worry too much about internal politics and double dealing and don't do enough for the people who elect them. The independents don't get caught up with the caucus system of the major parties. We vote according to our conscience and don't go around the corridors of parliament canvassing votes.' He also spoke harshly of the Gray Government in the lead-up to the election, claiming Robin Gray had tried to trick the electorate into believing Wesley Vale would have created jobs and the Greens were to blame.

Gray was consistently labelling the 'greenies' as extremists who were not willing to compromise. He told the annual conference of the Australian Petroleum Exploration Association (APEA) just prior to the election that, 'As developers of the nation's resources you must show the people of Australia that you, not the greenies, are providing the inheritance of future generations. The high moral ground sits much better with the people who create the jobs and build the wealth than it does with those who've never created a job in their lives and view profits as the wages of sin.'

Among the editorial comment to appear as the election results became clearer, *Sydney Morning Herald* columnist Robert Haupt spoke of the near religious reverence being attributed to Brown and Milne at the Hobart Town Hall campaign launch:

> No-one cried Hallelujah, but make no mistake, it was a revival meeting . . . At what other rally would a politician have won a cheer with a line like this? 'Any de-inking of recycled materials must not involve organochlorides.' It raises the rafters in the Tasmanian house of environmental purity (Hobart diocese) . . . Perhaps there is only a certain amount of credulity to go around. There is no doubt members of the Tasmanian establishment have exhausted theirs: 'The Hydro', Kafkaesque society that ran, in self-perpetuity, the key elements of the Tasmanian economy for many decades without scrutiny, is more or less dead.

Richard Flanagan later branded Haupt the 'Kylie Minogue of political journalism'.

Bob Brown, the man who had only months before stated to the national press that he hoped his future would not be in politics, was now set to become the leader of the first environmental grouping in Australia to form a coalition government.

Of their Chapter 9
own accord

asmania was fast transforming itself from the 'backward, sleepy hollow' tag it still wore in the eyes of many Australians, to being at the forefront of a paradigm shift with global implications. Bob Brown had made Australian electoral history by leading a loose, independent environmental grouping to the very brink of direct access to governmental power. The Green independents, not yet registered as an independent political party, won five seats at the 1989 Tasmanian election, denying either party a clear majority.

Bob Brown was at the centre of that transformation.

The five elected Green independent members consisted of old hands Bob Brown and Gerry Bates, two female teachers—Christine Milne and Di Hollister—and the Reverend Lance Armstrong, who had led a river clean-up campaign in Launceston.

Some of the candidates had needed coaxing from Brown in order to run. 'I must say that many of the best Green candidates are those who are most reluctant,' says Brown. 'We do need more people in politics who simply aren't getting into it for the ego trip that's involved or the kudos . . . That's one good thing I've enjoyed about the Green company . . . in the parliament: that they've been there for the Green cause, for the long-term vision that they have, for the impact that they can have rather than as self-serving politicians.'

Brown immediately described the extraordinary result as 'a great victory for the environment'. It was fifteen years since he had first run with the UTG and scored just 184 votes. Now there seemed to be no stopping him, he had polled at 23.5 per cent of primary votes, second only to Robin Gray.

After the election, Brown compared the rise of the Greens to the rise of the labour movement a century ago. 'The planetary environment is enduring enormous problems and people have become aware that the onus is on us to do something,' he told the media after the result was announced. 'The conventional political wisdom has been that environment issues are episodic and that once they are over they are forgotten. That thinking should have ended in Tasmania on Saturday.'

Not quite. Behind the scenes, leading businessman and newspaper entrepreneur Edmund Rouse, 63 at the time, offered a $110 000 bribe to ALP member Jim Cox to cross the floor and join Robin Gray's coalition. The move would have given Gray the numbers he needed. 'It cannot be underestimated, the emnity with which the Greens were viewed, as far as the establishment in Hobart was concerned,' says Brown. 'But there it is. We had people willing to go to those lengths to stop the Greens getting into power.' The move backfired, and Rouse was subsequently gaoled.

Gray hoped the independents would form a coalition with him, although he conceded it would be difficult to work with Dr Brown 'given his support for things such as legalisation of homosexuality and the opposition he has to many developments'.

Brown describes a meeting with Robin Gray where the Premier's assistant lit endless cigarettes and handed them to his boss, while Christine Milne, at the time suffering from bronchitis, suffered quietly in the background until Gerry Bates pointedly flung open a window. The outcome of the meeting was that, in short, Gray was not comfortable with the independents playing a significant role in government policy determination.

Unrattled, the Green independents met with the leader of the Tasmanian ALP, Michael Field, and negotiated the unprecedented Green–ALP accord. This meant that the ALP would form a minority government, under policy terms dictated by the Green independents.

The broad outlines of the accord included the commitment that the Green independents and the ALP would work together to 'create a more open, community-responsive style of government', and 'introduce much needed social, economic, environmental and parliamentary reforms to Tasmania'.

More specifically, the Douglas-Apsley National Park, the Huon forests, the Denison/Spires area, Hartz Mountains, and Little Fisher Valley areas were to be protected. The Wesley Vale pulp mill would not go ahead. Areas to be immediately added to World Heritage listing would include the Central Plateau, Campbell River, Eldon Range, and Lower Gordon River. Current logging operations in East Picton, Jackeys Marsh and Lake Ina would cease. The Forestry Commission was to be subject to a full review, and any National Estate areas judged non-essential to the logging industry would be protected as national parks. Notably, in its agenda for reform, the ALP supported decriminalising homosexual acts between consenting adults in private, although this would be subject to a free vote by party members.

It amounted to nothing less than a complete reversal of the direction of Tasmanian governance.

By 1 June 1989 the Hobart *Mercury* was already in panic mode. Its editorial line followed, 'The imposition in full of an extreme conservationist's land use philosophy in Tasmania would have catastrophic effects on the state's economy'. Premier Gray, his leadership of the state in the balance, flew to Melbourne to seek the support of right-wing unions to smash the accord—to no avail.

The Green independents were getting everything they could through this rare window of opportunity. The accord basically followed the policies they had set out in their election campaign. The last provision to get pushed through was that a liquor allowance for ministers of religion be dropped. It was dropped.

Bob Brown put the successful motion of no confidence in Robin Gray on 30 June 1989. Robin Gray was bitter. He accused Brown personally of being 'a master of distortion and an environmental zealot', adding that Brown used to be a man of principle, but he was now a numbers man. Gray added that the Greens wanted to turn the state of Tasmania into 'some sort of guinea pig for the philosophies of Dr Brown and the Green movement'.

For a time, the accord appeared to be working. 'The dream of the United Tasmania Group that they could in some way grab the middle ground—the power—and influence the course of events had come true twenty years later,' says Brown. He knew that every forest the Green independents could save now would save decades of campaign work later.

Brown and Milne frequently travelled around the state, meeting union leaders and local people. 'Local people no longer want the kind of bitterness that existed in the past,' said Milne. 'They want input into the decision making process.' Brown pushed the line that the Green independents brought no threat to jobs, but that the future lay in tourist industries. 'This is a new era,' he said. 'The important thing is that communities have been brought back into politics, back to the discussion.'

Bob Brown had now acquired an international reputation, and was frequently invited to address groups all over the world. He took a trip to Washington in April 1990 to accept the Goldman environmental prize, an award given to individuals identified as having made an outstanding contribution to advancing environmental protection. He used the opportunity to criticise the Bush (senior) administration, telling the US media that instead of factoring every environmental decision against the economic costs, 'really it's the other way around. Any economic decision should be environmentally costed.' He also used the limelight to speak of politicians who are motivated primarily on economic concerns, saying that they would soon find themselves swept away on a 'green tide'.

His comments came just as the Bush administration was announcing its rejection of international pressure to take a more vigilant stance on curbing greenhouse emissions. Brown was broadening his field to that of an international political figure.

In Canberra, the green spirit was catching. The ALP won a third term of office; Prime Minister Bob Hawke and Senator Graham Richardson were talking up the environment. Brown stridently noted that, 'From here on in, every election is going to have green policies right up front, in every party going into elections—and that's going to be a hallmark of Australian and world politics as we go into the next century'. He added that the Tasmanian election results had been broadcast right throughout Europe and 'added to the optimism that the whole world is going green'.

While Graham Richardson did not quite share Brown's ebullience, he also noted that the environment 'is not an issue that will go away because the economy is at the forefront of people's thinking . . . rather the environment will become even more important because of it'. He further predicted that the environment would be the big decision-maker for people in elections throughout the next decade.

Meanwhile, Bob's friend and Hobart housemate Judy Henderson was visiting Oxford in June 1990, as the Chair of

Community Aid Abroad. She got a phone call from Hobart and knew something was up.

Bob's voice immediately sounded animated down the phone line. Two large bush blocks had come on the market in the Liffey Valley, just behind Bob's place, and the woodchippers had their sights set on them. Bob told Henderson he intended to place a bid for the blocks. It seemed the only way to save them from the woodchippers. She counselled caution, knowing full well that Bob didn't have the money.

Within a week, Henderson received a second phone call. Bob had sent a bidder to the auction. His bidder had successfully placed the highest bid on the blocks—$250 000. 'The next thing I got a phone call saying, "Well, I've bought those blocks",' recalls Henderson. 'I asked him how he was going to pay for them. He said: "I really don't know, Judy".'

Over the next month Bob managed to convince his bank manager to make the massive loan. 'I found that extraordinary,' says Henderson. 'He had no collateral, so how he managed to convince the bank I don't know to this day.'

He did have the Goldman prize money he'd just received in America. Brown put the entire $50 000 prize toward the deposit on the two blocks, and set in motion what was to become the establishment of the Australian Bush Heritage Fund. Bob recalls that after he had made the successful bid, he was told by the auctioneer that they received a phone call from Northern Woodchips (the company that was later to become Gunns Limited) that very same night. The woodchip company knew there was $400 000 worth of woodchips on the blocks, so they had missed out on a guaranteed profit of $150 000. The rep from Northern Woodchips reportedly asked the auctioneer about the successful bidder—'Was it *that* Doctor Brown?'.

With Bob busy in the Tasmanian Parliament, a Bush Heritage Fund management committee was established, and fundraising experts were brought in from interstate. 'In fact, we always laugh and say Bob has the ideas, and then he just handballs them to someone else,' quips Henderson. 'We got fundraisers down from Sydney, set up a management committee, drew up a constitution, and became an incorporated institution.'

Henderson later became the Chair of Australian Ethical Investment Ltd, and says: 'I remember joking about it later, that the subsequent investment policies never would have allowed that decision to take over the loan. The only security was the timber of the block, so if we'd gone bankrupt, we would have had to sell the blocks to be woodchipped in order to pay off the loan.'

Bob approached a number of individuals, including journalist and broadcaster Phillip Adams, pianist Roger Woodward and former West Australian Greens leader Jo Vallentine to become public patrons of the project. 'We all supported Bob in this because we felt the time was right, and that this was something that would capture the attention of more "light green" conservationists who wanted to do something tangible for the environment,' says Henderson. 'But we struggled for a long time, and there were a lot of people who put personal money into it, at great personal risk.'

Throughout the 1990s and right up to the present day, the Australian Bush Heritage Fund has gone on to become one of the most successful environmental initiatives in recent Australian history, having acquired close to a million acres of bushland around Australia.

Meanwhile, Bob was facing his toughest tests yet back in the Tasmanian Parliament. Despite significant environmental achievements throughout the fifteen months of the accord, including a doubling of the size of south-western Tasmanian World Heritage wilderness—the Green–ALP accord fell apart in October 1990, when the ALP failed to honour the agreed-upon limits for woodchipping in native forests.

Brown had warned Premier Michael Field that this would be the outcome if he followed the new line of resource security the ALP had adopted. The resource security legislation pursued by the Field Government handed control of all unprotected Tasmanian forests over to a small number of logging companies for the next fifteen years.

It was a significant litmus test, demonstrating clearly that the Greens would sooner bring down a government than sell themselves short. After the accord fell apart, the Green independents proved that the ALP was now in a volatile state as a minority government. They voted with the Opposition on a number of issues, notably trimming a list of schools earmarked by the ALP for closure right back to almost half the original number.

Brown says that throughout this period the pressure was building on the ALP, as unemployment was growing rapidly with logging industries moving toward increased mechanisation. Massive 'anti-greenie' demonstrations came to Hobart, with logging companies busing people in from all over the state. Brown says he welcomed logging contractors in his office after they had received no positive assurances from the premier, the Forestry minister, or the Forestry Commission. 'We agreed at the outset . . . we won't talk about the forests because we might find disagreement there. But these men were all heavily mortgaged with their logging trucks . . . and were faced with zero income.'

The logging company North Broken Hill was shedding logging contractors and, according to Brown, 'in the boom and bust cycle of the woodchipping industry, they were the victims'.

Brown says he had been advocating right throughout his term in parliament that the companies should underwrite contractors, so they didn't carry all the capital investment risk. 'They worked prodigious hours—up at four in the morning, often home at night just in time to go to bed—and had given these companies enormous service. They were abandoned not only by the companies but by their political representatives.'

Brown says he had extensive discussions with the contractors on how to register with the public that they had been unfairly treated, 'and hopefully gain some sympathy within the ALP'.

Instead, the ALP introduced resource security legislation in 1991, supported by the Gray Opposition, guaranteeing the logging companies continuing access to the forests. It was the straw that broke the camel's back as far the Green independents were concerned. Field knew by this stage that the Green independents would immediately pass a motion of no confidence in him and bring down the government. In a phone call just minutes before he put the resource security bill, Premier Field told Brown it had been a dream of his in politics to give the forest industries this kind of security.

Jim Bacon, then of the Tasmanian Trades and Labour Council, was something of an intermediary between Michael Field and Robin Gray throughout this period. Brown said he met with Bacon in his office and looked him square in the eye and told him that resource security was not going to deliver jobs to forest workers. Bacon, Field and Gray all felt that resource security was absolutely the way to go, and the Green independents couldn't stop them. Jim Bacon went on to become the ALP Premier of Tasmania at the beginning of the new millennium, a time when woodchipping is advancing at an unprecedented pace in the state's history.

'It was far too much for us in conscience to be able to wear,' said Brown. The five Green independents joined the crossbench, but agreed to support the Field Government in so far as at least getting the Budget through. The media and the Liberals pounced on the breakdown of the accord as firm evidence that minority governments are doomed, but in hindsight, the period of the Green–ALP Accord was in some ways the most progressive period in Tasmania's recent history.

❧ ❧ ❧

By October 1990, newspapers around the country were having a field day with the breakdown of the accord. 'Green Pact Fails' headlined the *Age* on 2 October, 'Labor on the Brink'. The *Australian Financial Review* chipped in with the headline, 'Wither the Greens?' in which it suggested Kermit the Frog's theme song, 'It's not easy being green' as a fitting tune to sum up the fate of the Tasmanian Greens. The paper claimed the demise raised the troublesome question 'of whether green groups anywhere are capable of winning and retaining political power . . . The breakdown has left not only the Greens in despair. It has left Tasmania with an unstable minority government capable of being forced into an election at any moment, brought business confidence to an all-time low and forced Greens around the world to ask where they can head next.'

Premier Field described the breakdown of the accord as more of a separation than a divorce, suggesting that the two parties would continue to work together. Brown went further, saying that the government's honour was gone after it had failed to live up to the obligations of the accord, and that the government was now 'on notice'. Brown persisted that the fifteen months of the accord had revealed how green groups within a hung parliament can change the course of history.

A no-confidence motion wasn't put until 30 October 1991, when the Field Government finally attempted to put its resource security legislation through the parliament. Brown declared to the packed House and gallery that he and his Green independent colleagues were proudly defiant to protect 'not only this magnificent house of ours but . . . to stop the further degradation of the planet'. He said the accord had set out to protect not only the forests, but also the jobs of workers in the forest industry, but that resource security would allow North Broken Hill to export some of Tasmania's World Heritage forests as woodchips.

In a political move that bought the Green independents time and saved the ALP for the short term, the Green independents then supported the government's ability to control parliament through an adjournment motion. The resource security legislation had been defeated for the life of the parliament. Gray's Opposition was still left empty-handed, after having voted with the Greens in the hope of securing government. The no-confidence motion was deemed by Field 'ambiguous and conditional, and not an unqualified vote of no confidence in my government'. Mr Gray later offered to reverse his position and back the resource security motion, but Premier Field said, 'How can you trust a man who has done four backflips in four days?'.

By January 1992, with another election in sight, the Green independents ran candidates in all 35 Tasmanian seats. Both parties were urging Tasmanian voters to elect a major-party majority to avoid the 'instability' caused by the Green independents. As the election results came through in February, the Greens' support had slipped to 12.8 per cent across the state. Brown's vote in Denison was almost halved. Labor lost the election by a landslide. Former premier Field said of the Green independents, 'If you want to express belief you join a church. Most of their [Greens] appeal is emotive and their structure is authoritarian.'

According to Brown, the accord had demonstrated that there was no real difference between the two major parties. 'In some sense, it has also increased the community's awareness that the choice is now either between the Greens or what we call the Laborals.'

As the dust settled, greens all over Australia were gathering to set up a new national Greens party. Bob Brown, who was now president of the incorporated Bush Heritage Fund and had recently been named Australian of the Decade by the *Australian*, was the obvious choice to be its leader.

Green Chapter 10 *and gay*

While the fledgling Green party in Tasmania had made such a remarkable ascendancy, there were others in the state that had noted Bob Brown's personal style and leadership with more than a passing interest.

Bob Brown had gone through a remarkably traumatic ordeal coming to terms with his sexuality throughout the 1950s and 1960s. He was now widely recognised within Tasmanian society and nationally as a gay man who had led one of the most successful environmental battles in the nation's history, and taken his convictions directly into the political sphere.

It is all the more remarkable that Brown was able to achieve such political victories while remaining relatively up-front about his sexuality, in a state of Australia where being gay was still against the law. Yet an image of the asexual saintly Bob was one that effectively engaged the mainstream media. Here was a man whose cause—that of Tasmanian forest protection and the wider political dimensions of leading the Australian Greens—eclipsed his sexuality in the nation's eyes.

Brown emerged from a very different era in Australian history, a time when homosexuality carried much more of a stigma than it does today, and sexuality itself was rarely publicly discussed. Although Brown has never denied or hidden his sexuality in the public political arena, he chose from early on not to make issues around homosexuality or gay law reform central to his public political persona.

After matter-of-fact announcements of his homosexuality in maiden speeches to both the Tasmanian and later the national parliament, Bob Brown has never placed himself in the public eye as a gay rights campaigner. In his first speech to the federal Senate in 1996, he noted: 'some twenty years ago I, as that young doctor in Launceston, made it public that I am homosexual. Now twenty years down the line much has changed but I, naturally, have not.'

In the context of the rise of the Greens, its agenda would be fairly narrow if Bob Brown as party leader were to make sexuality his primary focus. Moreover, Bob Brown never seemed to be comfortable confronting his parents, Jack and Marjorie, with his sexuality in too forthright a manner. He never had an open relationship with another man while his parents were alive.

There is perhaps a sense that Bob's desire to keep any overt display of his sexuality out of his parents' gaze meant that he was never able to fully come to terms with his own sexuality.

'I don't believe he did lead a full life, at least not a sexual life, until his parents were out of the picture,' says Peter Thompson. 'He knew it would have a hurtful impact on them. He was very cautious about it, and really preferred it was contained from them. It wasn't "Oh gee, what are my parents going to think"—like a child. I think it was more of a mature sensibility,' he says. 'The more important point is what it was doing to him as a person and expressing who he was. I think it held him back—held him up, if you like. I think it diminished his life to some extent.'

Judy Henderson says she and Bob grew up in a very different world. 'It wasn't something that we were even aware of when we were teenagers,' she says. 'I wouldn't have recognised it even if I knew about it back then. He had very good friends among the boys in the class, but he was very good-looking and equally popular among the girls.'

The first Henderson knew of Bob's sexuality was when he came back from his trip to England in 1970, when he came to visit her in Perth and let her know in person that he was homosexual. She was one of the first people he summoned the courage to come out to in Australia.

'The subject of Bob's sexuality was never raised with Jack Brown directly, to my knowledge,' says Henderson. 'He clearly had known, because it had been in the public arena before then, but it was just never talked about.'

There was even a presumption, both on Jack's part and, on occasion, in the media, that Judy Henderson and Bob Brown were an 'item'. Having a female companion, even a platonic one, seemed to make the issue of Bob's sexuality easier to avoid, at least from his father's perspective.

'The fact that I was there made it all alright. It was a non-issue,' says Henderson. 'Bob would say that concern for the family was not the issue. That it was just the pressure of public office. But I think it was also that he was very aware of the stigma and how it might upset his family. His family were always extremely supportive of everything he did. Jack was wonderful, I adored him. But he was the product of an era, and you just didn't talk about these things, they didn't exist. Bob, out of respect for his father, wasn't going to confront him with it.'

'It's very difficult for anyone in a public position to have a relationship. The pressure on Bob to constantly perform in the parliament—there was no opportunity for him to even think about a personal life.'

Henderson says that Bob never shied away from his homosexuality if asked, and the great respect many Australians felt for him (evidenced in his being awarded Australian of the Year) gave him 'oxygen' to keep going throughout the years prior to 1996, without the support of an intimate partner.

However, it has been evident in the past decade that Brown has reached a new buoyancy in matters concerning going public on sexuality issues. This is in no small part due to what he called 'being set free out of a prison' on finding a loving relationship with partner Paul Thomas. Before Thomas, Brown had never maintained an ongoing intimate relationship. The reasons for this are difficult to define, although Brown has always maintained that the demands of public office made having any personal life near-impossible.

'I think I'd be far less optimistic and content with giving a huge commitment to public life [if not for Paul],' said Bob in a *Good Weekend* interview.

> He said early on that we owe it to each other to be in touch once a day. If I'm awake at 3 o'clock in the morning in a motel room and the going's rough, I can give him a call and he doesn't mind. Fortunately, he goes straight back to sleep . . .
>
> I think we have something to give the world, and that something is enlarged by the fact of what we've got to give each other.

In 1988 Paul Thomas called the first meeting that led to the eventual victory of gay law reform in Tasmania. It is fitting that Bob Brown met Paul at that first meeting, where he was invited as guest speaker.

Paul Thomas—born in 1955, the first of seven children— is a gentle, rural-born Tasmanian from a sheep and beef farming family. He runs a Tibetan rug shop in central Hobart today. Thomas says he also went through hell in coming to terms with his sexuality, thwarting the expectations of his devoutly Catholic family to continue a farming tradition. He even attended a mainland agricultural college before determining a different career path.

Thomas was every bit the easygoing, hardworking, good-looking, and sporty, popular schoolboy—former captain of his school Aussie Rules footy team. He was almost the classic portrait of a typical heterosexual. Except that he was gay and, like so many Tasmanian gays, disguised and cloaked his homosexual longings—with damaging personal consequences.

Unlike Bob Brown, Thomas even had a number of girl-friends in his twenties, although his 'awareness' of sexuality made him unwilling to commit to serious relationships with them. Between the ages of 25 and 30 Thomas had encounters with a number of men, all of them married or 'straight-acting'—he never met a single openly gay person until he was 30, when he left Australia for New Zealand in February 1985 in an effort to 'sort himself out'.

'I went to New Zealand on my own for a "holiday", but in reality to escape some complex relationship entanglements. At that point in time I knew of men willing to have physical intimacy but knew of no openly gay people, even though I was 30 years of age. I had a fantastic time coming to terms with my sexuality in the company of a friendly well-adjusted gay community in New Zealand,' says Thomas.

Thomas is ten years younger than Bob, bearded and hand-some, and displaying a remarkable generosity of spirit, evident even on first meeting. He has been instrumental in setting up a number of gay and lesbian support networks in Tasmania. These include GUSTO (Gay University Students of Tasmania Organisation) set up after his return to Tasmania from New Zealand. He was a founding member of the Tasmanian AIDs Council, and assisted in the establishment of a Gay Informa-tion Line.

Thomas recalls, 'In early 1988 I established a gay aware-ness group and organised a series of discussion evenings. The second such discussion topic was "Gay Politics, Law Reform" and I invited Bob along as the guest speaker.'

Although Thomas had been a fan of Bob for many years, the gay law reform meetings were the first time they actually met. 'I had been a silent admirer since he commenced campaigning for the Franklin River and his "coming out" on national television some years earlier. The issues raised at that meeting were such that a "group of ten" decided . . . to meet again in a fortnight at which the TGLRG [Tasmanian Gay and Lesbian Rights Group] was formed . . . After taking some time to think it through, Rodney Croome and Nick Toonen decided to be the spokespersons for the group,' said Thomas.

It wasn't until the mid-1990s that Paul Thomas moved toward becoming Brown's partner. At the age of 51, Brown was able to find in Thomas the very thing that had eluded and tormented him for much of his adult life—a loving male companion.

Come 1996, Bob Brown and Paul Thomas transformed what had previously been an activist-based working relationship into the romantic sphere when they took a forest walk together on the eve of Brown's return to politics as a Tasmanian senator. Thomas had been a campaign worker for Brown throughout that election campaign.

'When I first started to get to know Bob, I had just come out of a relationship, so at that time I was sort of available,' said Thomas in the *Good Weekend* interview. 'I had met Bob in passing a number of times, but our life circumstances weren't conducive to forming a relationship. On election day, when I grabbed Bob and took him away from all the pressure and we had a walk in the bush, I think we both realised we were going to have a significant friendship.'

'The personal contact just confirmed all the positive things I'd heard and read over many years: very sincere, interested in you as a person, no pretentiousness at all because of his profile, a natural, likeable sort of person. Our relationship has never been threatened. I guess the core of it is companionship. It's very easy to have a relationship with Bob. In the years we've been together, Bob and I have never had a fight.'

The two men exchanged rings from a street merchant in Indonesia, rings they still wear today. 'We were on the beach at Lombok and a young fellow pushed us very hard to buy,' recalled Brown. 'It was just a mutual thing where we agreed to get two and give one to each other. After we bought them for $20, the fellow broke down and cried because the sale meant he wouldn't be beaten by his employer and had enough money to buy food. So out of our mutual exchange, some extra benefit happened. I'd like to see that also as a cameo of what our relationship is about.'

Brown has also spoken of the initial misgivings he felt in entering into a relationship—the impact it might have on his capacity to focus on politics. He says he felt inherently vulnerable to discrimination up until the time he started seeing Paul, but that the relationship has given him great personal strength and endurance.

He has said that his 'centre of gravity' has shifted from his lone cottage in Liffey to his companion Paul. The Liffey cottage, with its sign out the front gate saying 'Trespassers Welcome' is Brown's personal hideaway in the country without a computer or electricity, designed as a site to focus primarily on environmental activism. In Paul Thomas, Brown has found a much more invigorating centre of gravity.

❧ ❧ ❧

From early in his political career, Brown has evidently placed other political issues, specifically environmentalism, above sexuality issues as the cause he was willing to champion. In fact, early in the piece, when questioned on his relative silence regarding gay rights, Brown would quip, 'There's no point having gay law reform when there's no planet to live on' or words to that effect. It is a rather reductionist position that Bob Brown certainly wouldn't posit today.

Tasmanian gay rights campaigner Rodney Croome says that Bob Brown's journey, from his coming out as gay to his environmental work, has been mirrored in the broader Tasmanian community.

'His former sexual politics were almost apologetic,' said Croome. 'He said "I'm not proud", and that wasn't an issue he wanted to talk about. By the time we get to law reform in 1997 he has changed his position to say that sexual diversity is a good thing, and that the society is poorer without it. His sense of himself changes as Tasmania changes.'

Other friends of Brown say this image of Bob Brown being silent and apologetic about his gayness is inaccurate and that his actions—specifically putting gay law reform to the Tasmanian Parliament in the 1980s—demonstrated otherwise. But it is clear that by the dawn of the new millennium, Bob Brown was a much more willing spokesperson when questioned on gay issues. Although he still chooses to shy away from overt displays of his sexuality, this is surely more to do with his personal style rather than any lack of conviction. Brown has contributed to a number of national gay and lesbian compilations in the past years, and even became one of the popular gay magazine *DNA*'s 'ten most intriguing gay people' for 2002.

It is vital to keep in mind the vastly different world Bob Brown came from when he was a young man grappling with his sexuality. There was no Mardi Gras, no commercial gay culture stretching across Australian cities, no gay visibility whatsoever in Tasmania.

'Night after night I pleaded with Jesus to make me normal,' he wrote in his essay 'Keeping a Promise', recalling the struggle he encountered with his sexuality at the age of nineteen in Sydney. When that didn't help, he turned to more obscure means of attempting to medically 'cure' his sexual longings.

Brown recalls that a Sydney psychiatrist was the first person to whom he confessed that he was gay. The psychiatrist 'turned out not to be the most warm-hearted person' recalled Brown.

'With the subtlety of a bulldozer, he asked if my mother was domineering (no, she wasn't), if I hated my father (no, I didn't) and other such questions. Then, to my consternation, he told me to turn around and drop my trousers and underpants.' The psychiatrist then gave Brown a shot of testosterone into the right cheek of his backside and instructed him to come back each week for more shots. The doctor further instructed him to read Van der Velde's book on heterosexual sex. Brown says the ordeal left him feeling sad and alone—'forsaken by the same God that made me gay, suicide beckoned,' he wrote.

What followed were years of 'private hell' as Brown went through medical school in Sydney, still isolated and silent on his sexuality, and subjected himself to the early Australian trials of a radical treatment called 'aversion therapy'.

Within weeks I was sitting in a chair, while my reaction to photos of nudes projected onto a screen was measured. My hands were wired to an electric shock machine. Each male on the screen was followed by a shock. The occasional female was followed by the relief of no shock at all and, sometimes, a sip of water . . . Although I was ashamed of the treatment, the doctors were non-judgmental . . . Inside I was dying away.

It is a telling footnote to Brown's eventual survival and personal style that in 1976 at the age of 32, as a Launceston doctor, he decided that the best way to tell the world he was gay was to start by knocking on the doors of his neighbours in Liffey. He informed the mainly Baptist families in the area that he was homosexual, before announcing it in public forums such as national television and Tasmanian newspapers.

In June of 1976 Bob Brown went public with his homosexuality when he appeared on *This Day Tonight* stating his sexual orientation. In the months prior to that he had informed his closest group of friends. The television appearance sparked an article in the Launceston *Examiner* on 10 June that ran on page three under the headline, 'Doctor says he's gay'. However, a caption on the front page, complete with a picture of Brown, read 'Doctor's Brave Plea—In a courageous plea for homosexual law reform, a well-known northern Tasmanian doctor admitted that he is a homosexual'.

In one gutsy swoop, the word was out.

But as Rodney Croome suggests, at this point Bob was certainly not yet claiming to be proud of his sexual orientation. The *Examiner* story quoted Brown saying, 'The fact that I am a homosexual gives me no feeling of pride. It's just a situation that exists.' The article was framed in the context of Brown making the disclosure in order to help put pressure on the government to bring about gay law reform in Tasmania. 'I feel I have reached a position of security from which I have an obligation to help the less fortunate,' he said.

The article also declared that Bob Brown was the first Tasmanian of note to publicly announce himself as gay. Throughout the 1970s in Tasmania, people were still liable for arrest on the grounds of homosexuality.

Other quotes from Brown in the article shed light on his own personal struggle with his sexuality throughout his twenties: 'Many young people are going through a great deal of trauma over something for which they are not to blame,' he said. 'None of them can adjust and enjoy life as much as if they were not homosexuals. They are in a unique situation in the community because, through years of guilt and self-regret, they can turn to no-one.'

By the following Monday, letters had started appearing in the paper, the first under the heading 'It's in the Bible', drawing readers' attention to some interesting reading in the Old Testament book of Leviticus on the subject. The next day the entire Letters section was headed 'Homosexuals'. A correspondent from Deviot wrote that she 'strongly question[ed] the claim that homosexuals are born that way'. 'Let us honestly admit that the blame lies at the door of our perverted society.'

Another writer, under the pen-name CONCERNED from Deviot, took issue with the newspaper using the word 'gay'. 'I consider it reprehensible and irresponsible that in reporting the circumstances of Dr Brown's courageous announcement on his unfortunate biological abnormality, the label "gay" with its connotation of derision should be used.' It gives a telling indication of the changing times.

The Franklin campaign was the point that perhaps irrevo-cably entwined the personal development of Bob Brown, including the inseparable presence of his sexual journey—with his emergence as a unifying national symbol for the green movement. Brown wrote of that voyage down the Franklin, and how it intersected with his own doubts over his sexuality. In a moment of triumphant epiphany, Brown told Paul Smith before undertaking the journey that he was gay, and was met with an unfazed reaction. This came at a time when gay liber-ation in Tasmania was still a distant dream, when any mention of homosexuality was outlawed in the state's education system.

'A forester asked me if I would raft the Franklin River with him,' Brown wrote. 'I was 30 and had enough sense to know such a risky undertaking meant we had total confidence in each other. So, I told him I was homosexual. He was nonplussed. "Well," he said, "I'm not even remotely homo-sexual. I can recognise a good looking guy just as I can pick out a good trout, but that's about it." The trip was so great that it affirmed my conviction to save our environment, thereby changing my life forever,' wrote Brown.

Even after his first public declaration that he was gay in 1976, throughout the Franklin campaign, in which he was a leading figure, Brown was generally portrayed as an asexual monastic type figure whose former zeal for Presbyterianism had found a new focus in environmental activism. He did little to counter the perception.

However, there were many young homosexuals in Tasmania who had noted Brown's public coming-out with more than a passing interest. Rodney Croome is a fifth-generation Tasmanian who grew up on a dairy farm in Sheffield and later moved to Devonport. Like many Tasmanian activists, Croome came from a conservative background, and similarly to Brown, this presented him with massive hurdles. For Croome and other Tasmanian gay rights campaigners—including Nick Toonen and Paul Thomas—Bob Brown and the Tasmanian Greens provided a prototype of how they would frame their own political battle. They filled a bus and travelled around Tasmania to promote their law reform message in a mobilisation that is not altogether dissimilar to the US freedom rides.

'When I came out it in the early to mid-80s it was still a big thing,' said Croome. 'If you had any desire to live a happy life and you were gay or lesbian you left Tasmania. If you stayed you accepted a very strict regime of closetedness.'

Croome says that many Tasmanians—not out of bigotry, just out of ignorance—didn't think there were any gay Tasmanians. 'But like quite a few other people at that time in Tasmania, I decided that I wasn't going to be turned into a sexual refugee. I'd seen those people at Mardi Gras from Tasmania saying, "We had to leave twenty years ago" and the tears . . . streaming down their faces. I decided early on that I didn't want to be one of those people. We realised that we couldn't stay here and be who we wanted to be without radical change. We had no choice but to make sure that things changed radically. We perceived this very early on because the limits on our lives were so strict. We set about creating a new kind of gay community and a new kind of Tasmania.'

In the rural and industrial northern parts of Tasmania—particularly around Burnie, Devonport and Ulverstone, there was a strong reactionary movement brewing against the state electoral success of the Greens.

In an unprecedented mobilisation, residents of these towns formed groups to stage street demonstrations opposing gay law reform, and discredit the Greens—the party led by a known homosexual. There is a direct link here between the

Greens' own campaign techniques and the methods later employed by Tasmanian anti-gay groups. Christine Milne had created a group to oppose pulp mill development around Devonport called CROPS (Concerned Residents Against Pulp Mills). Then in the early 1990s, an alter ego of this group formed under the name CRAMP (Concerned Residents Against Moral Pollution) specifically to oppose gay law reform.

Croome says that although Brown was very cautious at the first meetings of what was to become the Tasmanian gay and lesbian rights lobby, the Greens were certainly the biggest single source of inspiration the Tasmanian gay activists had to draw upon. He recalls that as a teenager he bought Peter Thompson's book *Bob Brown of the Franklin River* just for the two paragraphs right at the end that make mention of sexuality. He kept the book hidden under his bed just in case anyone thought he was gay, he says, 'or worse, a greenie'.

As one of the leaders of the mass gay law reform push in Tasmania, Croome says many of the techniques and activist philosophies adopted came straight from the example of the evolution of the Tasmanian Greens. 'I'd say without the Greens our movement would not have taken the shape it did, and it may not have even existed,' declares Croome.

'We learnt the importance of having that media profile, of going right into people's living rooms. This gay law reform issue was in newspapers and on television news every night for nine years ... Every Tasmanian had to think about it, and every Tasmanian had to arrive at a new and more mature position than they had before. The media work, the campaign work, the direct action, the creation of new images and new identities—it was all the effect of what the Greens had done in the ten years prior. The Greens opened up Tasmanian politics to change in a way that hadn't been there before.'

According to Croome, many of the commonalities between early Green activism around the Franklin and Lake Pedder issues, and the fledgling gay law reform movement, were the result of direct and personal crossovers.

'Many of the people I came out with had been involved in the Greens' early movements. They had learnt from that experience that Tasmanian society was not a stagnant one: that change was possible, and that radical change was possible. They transferred those new understandings of Tasmania to the gay and lesbian movement. We were inspired by the Greens to do what we did. For many the desire for change, the desire for justice—was transferred to another issue,' said Croome.

'That was the link, and as with so much else, Bob symbolised the link. He was the leader of the Greens and was also known to be gay. He was an inspiration not only to those who cared for the environment, but also to gay and lesbian Tasmanians. It's almost impossible to convey in words how much of an inspiration he was—because he was gay and because he was a successful activist.'

But another of the gay law reform activists, Nick Toonen, says that while Bob Brown was an inspiration, he was one among many.

'Bob was a great tactical and strategic adviser, and of course is an inspirational figure generally, including his own public coming out in Tasmania long before the TGLRG was established. He was a great inspiration, but I wouldn't say he was a major inspiration over and above others. The major inspiration for me was the group of people who got together in the late '80s, and Bob was one of these. They include Richard Hale and Rodney Croome.'

Croome and Toonen were a central part of the small group who organised the Tasmanian gay law reform movement that led to the now infamous political protests at the Salamanca Market in the early 1990s. The group clearly had lofty ambitions when Paul Thomas called that first meeting. Croome now says that they didn't quite know what they were up against—orchestrating some of the biggest acts of gay and lesbian civil disobedience in Australian history in a state where there had been 150 years of silence and denial of gay life.

Croome says Brown's initial attitude toward the group's ambitions was 'a bit pessimistic . . . He had tried to change the law a couple of years earlier and failed. He was aware in a way we weren't of the barriers that awaited us. He knew how vicious and brutal and bent on the destruction of gay and lesbian people that some Tasmanians were. That may sound dramatic, but I choose my words very carefully. We didn't know what viciousness and brutality awaited us, we just thought that people would respond immediately to rational argument. So Bob was a bit more pessimistic than us. But it didn't really matter what he said—he was there and he summed up everything we wanted. We soon learnt why he had been cautious,' said Croome.

The group's awakening to the brutality and resistance they would stir up in Tasmania came when the arrests started at Hobart's Salamanca Market. The first step came in September 1988 when the Hobart City Council banned the stall of the Tasmanian Gay and Lesbian Rights Group from the Saturday morning market. The council's Mayor at the time, Doone Kennedy, reportedly justified the ban by saying that there was one law for heterosexuals and another for gays at the council's 'family market'.

Anyone identified as a supporter of the group, including people signing a petition or displaying a pink triangle, was ordered to leave the market or face arrest for trespass. One hundred and thirty people were arrested over the following seven weeks after the ban was implemented, and consequently faced victimisation and harassment from Tasmanian police and small anti-gay groups within the community.

'In relation to police brutality,' says Nick Toonen, 'there were some homophobic and anti-Jewish police incidents'. 'However, overall the police didn't strike me as brutal, rather doing their job under difficult circumstances. There were threats of brutality at other events. I remember a group of youths' led by an older man, who had cricket bats and were being abusive and threatening at an anti-gay rally on the north-west coast. The abuse and brutality that was most significant were gay bashings away from the campaign—vulnerable individuals picked on and assaulted by others in malls, schools, streets etc. And also the brutal incitement to such acts by politicians and other community "leaders".'

However, in the subsequent months, all charges were dropped against those arrested for defying the ban, and the Tasmanian Government was facing increasing international pressure for reform from press reports as far away as Moscow and Washington. Again employing tactics that had been successful for the Greens over the Franklin, the Tasmanian Gay and Lesbian Rights Group knew they would have to seek support from outside Tasmania if the laws were ever to be changed. The gay law reform issue was suddenly on the news every night in Tasmania, moving the issue of homosexuality in Tasmania from the extreme margins of state, national and international discourse into a position of central and pivotal political significance.

'But that's only the beginning, that Salamanca incident,' says Croome. 'Throughout the late '80s and early '90s there were anti-gay rallies in Tasmania the likes of which have never been seen anywhere else in the world. It still makes me cringe now to think about it. The resistance we encountered was unbelievable, not necessarily from general Tasmanian society, but from segments of it, who feared the end of the world. They really did fear that their world was going to end with gay law reform . . . we're talking nine years of resistance that was only broken down through overwhelming popular support, and embarrassment that the rest of the world was laughing at Tasmania.'

Croome maintains it is a misconception to view the Tasmanian anti-gay movement as being purely religiously motivated; what the TGLRG faced was something altogether new and different.

'It was only in small part a religious movement. The anti-gay movement in Tasmania was a far-right secular movement that drew its techniques and ideas directly from the United States. This wasn't seen in other states—if you want to understand what we came up against and what Bob faced, you have to get rid of all those mainland preconceptions. Forget what you've read in the *Age* or the *Australian*. It's a new dynamic, new ideas—it's not the Festival of Light with a few posters—it was a threatening, far-right militant movement with frightening and radical goals. Bob knew that was there, we had no idea. They wanted us to disappear, we wanted them to dis-appear, and there was no compromise. It was a battle for Tasmania's soul. There was so much at stake.'

'But we took it on and we won—Tasmania has been transformed now,' says Croome.

From the Salamanca arrests into the early 1990s, the Tasmanian gay rights lobby kept fighting. Eventually, in 1994 the UN ruled that the Tasmanian Government was in breach of internationally recognised human rights codes for its failure to update laws relating to gays.

The newly appointed Tasmanian Greens leader Christine Milne eventually put the bill that was successful before the Tasmanian Parliament on 1 May 1997—and Tasmania went from having the most restrictive gay laws to adopting Australia's most progressive set of laws pertaining to gays and lesbians, including making seventeen the legal age of consent, on par with Tasmanian heterosexual consent laws. Rodney Croome reportedly wept after the decision was passed through the state parliament.

The long, hard-fought campaign, which had involved a successful appeal to the United Nations Human Rights Committee, a boycott of Tasmanian produce, the passage of the federal sexual privacy legislation and five attempts to get a bill through Tasmania's upper house, finally achieved a breakthrough on May Day, when the conservative opposition crumbled.

One of the main Tasmanian Liberal opponents of reform, the Legislative Council member George Brookes, told the

Council in debate that politicians had lost this round because the Greens held the balance of power with the minority Liberal Government. 'There will be other days,' he said. George Brookes has since been voted out of both the Legislative Council and Launceston City Council.

'I regard that as one of the greatest achievements of my political career to get [the bill] through both houses of the Tasmanian Parliament. It required a huge amount of political work,' said Milne, who led the Tasmanian Greens at that time, when the party held the balance of power in the state parliament.

'This decision lifts a destructive criminal stigma from our shoulders, a stigma we've lived with all our lives,' Rodney Croome told reporters gathered outside. 'It not only ends the gay decriminalisation campaign in Tasmania, it ends a 25-year campaign throughout Australia, because we were the last state. The passage of gay law reform is simply belated recognition of a much more profound change in community attitudes.'

While Bob Brown never placed himself at the centre of the Tasmanian gay law reform push, he did provide the movement with a catalyst—a potent inspiration in the form of a gay man in Tasmanian politics bringing about significant political change and dialogue way beyond the island.

'Everyone knew Bob was gay,' says Croome. 'But apart from his early attempts at law reform, he didn't really have much of a profile on gay issues—no-one did. There hadn't been that discussion in this state. There was a point in the mid-90s when the education system banned all discussion of homosexuality. We're talking about an establishment that had really deep interests in not acknowledging gay people.'

'That goes back to Tasmania's convict origins—to the association between homosexuality, convictism and subversion. It was very deep, very strong, and when people began to stand up and say this has to end, the response to that was very vicious and brutal. The establishment was happy to throw democratic conventions out the window in order to intimidate and imprison people. It went to all the lengths it possibly could. It's a state that's built in part on squashing gay and lesbian people.'

But Croome says that he also met people in Tasmania—heterosexual farmers or ordinary country people—who approached him and said they would like to support the push for gay law reform. He recalled one man of European origin approaching him in the streets at one of the confrontations between pro- and anti-gay reform activists saying, 'I don't want my kids to grow up in a place that treats people like that'.

'The other side of it is that Tasmania is not a wholly conservative society,' said Croome. 'It never has been, never will be. The way to characterise Tasmania is that it's a really deeply divided society—polarised. There was actually very popular support in Tasmania for gay law reform—much more than I've seen elsewhere. What we wanted—just little changes to the law—became a symbol of a better Tasmania, even if they weren't gay or didn't know anyone who was gay. Gay law reform became the place where all the tension and polarisation of Tasmania played itself out. Bob had so much moral authority, and he had that support behind him in this state, as a Green and as a gay man.'

❧ ❧ ❧

Paul Thomas is heavily involved in a number of political causes of his own, such as the Free Tibet campaign. He was an active Green local councillor for six years in the Huon Valley (south of Hobart) before retiring in October 2002. Thomas offers this explanation as to why neither he nor Brown have made sexuality the central issue on which they choose to base their politics. 'Bob is a Green who happens to be Pink not a Pink who happens to be Green!'

'Bob has always been an environmental campaigner. He just so happens to be gay. His initial support came as a result of his leadership in the Franklin campaign and has grown primarily for his stance on the environment. And more recently for the social justice principles of the Greens which is very much part of our platform, anti-decimation on all fronts being integral to Greens policy.'

'Bob was the first openly gay man elected to state government in Tasmania and I was the first openly gay man elected to local government in the state. Neither of us chose to campaign as gay activists as neither of us felt sexual identity to be central to our "cause", but neither have we ever hidden from it or not supported or worked for the interests of the gay community,' said Thomas.

Thomas is active in the Tasmanian branch of the Australia Tibet Council, and often hosts local environmental and social justice themed evenings at his Harrington Street shop premises. He is evidently affected by the current war in the Middle East and distributes information on the anti-war movement and does what he can to have a bigger impact through Bob.

It was Paul Thomas who had tentatively suggested to Bob the idea of putting to the Senate a motion of no confidence in John Howard over his lack of parliamentary or public consultation in deploying Australian troops to Iraq. Thomas said that Bob had considered the idea, done a bit of research on it, and decided it would be worth attempting. In the meantime, ALP party insiders had gotten wind of it and put the motion to the Senate where it was successful.

The motion of no confidence in John Howard was passed by the Senate and made front-page news nationally. Journalists often speak of the hidden influence of politicians' partners—here was the evidence—only with a slightly different bent in the case of Bob Brown and Paul Thomas.

Taking Chapter 11
it to the nation

In a café in the Sydney suburb of Newtown in 1992, a
meeting of environmental and peace activists from
Tasmania, New South Wales and Queensland resolved that
the time was right to establish the Australian Greens as an
official political party. There were no doubt many in the
Tasmanian Parliament delighted to see the back of Bob Brown
in February 1993 when he retired from the House of Assembly.

He had been a leading politician, surviving the turmoils of
state parliament for over a decade, demonstrating the ability
to effect change on a massive scale from the peripheral political footing of Tasmania. Had Brown stayed on in Tasmanian
Parliament for a further four years, he would have become
eligible for a superannuation payout of up to $900 000. But as
anyone close to Bob Brown can attest, money has never been
his primary motivator.

The Greens were going national and, as the most recognised environmental politician in the country, Bob would go
with them. Besides which, things had been turning dirty in the

Tasmanian Parliament, and the end of the Green–ALP accord had taken its toll. Brown was now approaching the age of 50.

As an example of the tactics Brown now had to endure, in April 1992 he was forced to admit that he had cut down trees on his Liffey property. The passionate anti-green MP Michael Hodgman brandished in parliament an old black and white photograph of stumps at Liffey, supplied by the previous owner of the property, John Dean. Brown's deceased father Jack was then quoted as saying, 'That . . . son of mine cut them down because he wanted a better view of the mountain'. In actual fact, the trees were introduced macrocarpa conifers, not natives.

Opposition from right-wing mining and forestry unions had become intense, particularly after the breakdown of the accord, which was frequently trumpeted as proof that the Greens, or any other minor party for that matter, should never be allowed such direct access to parliamentary power again.

Brown had increasingly sensed that his energies were better spent in an activist capacity, and he was keen to put his head down and do some environmental writing.

Just as the Field Labor Government (which had relied on the Greens to maintain its minority government) was voted out of office by the new Ray Groom-led Liberals, Brown was leading an anti-logging protest in the Picton, part of Tasmania's southern forests. He called on the newly appointed Paul Keating to intervene in the logging operation.

It was here at the Picton forest protests that Brown first got to know Ben Oquist, a 24-year-old Sydney student activist who had travelled to Tasmania with the express purpose of getting in touch with the Tasmanian Greens, and specifically Bob Brown. Oquist had just completed Communications and Media Studies at the University of Technology Sydney (UTS), and taking direct inspiration from the Tasmanian Greens, he had led a Greens ticket into the student elections. Oquist was elected as Australia's first Green student union president at UTS in 1991.

Oquist had joined the ALP when he was fourteen years old, but had grown disillusioned watching the Hawke/Keating years play out, and the environment being gradually pushed to the background of ALP policy priority. The Tasmanian Greens, says Oquist, were the only party in Australia at that time to energise him toward political activism, 'the only real inspiration on the political landscape'.

Oquist remembers watching the Greens' success in Tasmania on television with some excitement from his Sydney share house in 1989. He even held a special election night party on the night of the Tasmanian elections in which the Greens struck the Green–ALP accord. It was a pivotal moment for Oquist, a precursor to his becoming Bob Brown's longstanding personal assistant in 1996. When he travelled to Tasmania in 1991, Oquist didn't even know the Tasmanian Greens, although he had struck up initial contacts with Brown through his student union activities in Sydney. One of the key convictions Oquist shared with Brown was the need to nationalise the party.

'I felt the need for it, and lots of people were talking about a national Green party,' says Oquist. His support would become crucial in Sydney, where considerable opposition to the move existed in both conservation and socialist party circles.

'After the disappointment of ten years of the Labor government, it was obvious to me we needed a Green party. There was a feeling in the conservation movement that there was opposition to a Green party. I was surprised that hostility to the idea did exist strongly. I didn't understand why people wouldn't support that,' Oquist says.

But by the mid-1990s, the environment was slipping off the national agenda—it was no longer the hot potato it had been throughout the previous decade. No wonder then that when Ben Oquist organised a press conference in Sydney in August 1992 to announce the formation of the Australian Greens, the press didn't even bother turning up. The new Sydney Harbour Tunnel was dominating the news—a prophetic demonstration of the priorities of the media at that time, and of the challenges that would face the Australian Greens.

There had been building pressure for the Greens to form a national political party for many years. When leader of the German Greens Party, Petra Kelly came to Australia in 1984 she had spoken at length to people in the environment movement, including Jo Vallentine and Bob Brown (Kelly visited Brown in Liffey with her partner Gert Bastian in 1984) about the importance of nationalising the party.

Drew Hutton, who emerged as a leading Green out of anarchist and civil libertarian movements in Queensland, says that there were many factors slowing the formation of a united national Green party. In 1984, Hutton became one of the founders of the first Green party in Queensland, the Brisbane Green Party. It was the second political party in Australia officially named a 'green' party, after the New South Wales Greens formed a couple of months earlier, when the Sydney Greens took out the federal registration of the name 'The Australian Green Party'.

'Bob had a foothold in Tasmania, partly because of the Hare-Clark proportional representation system in place there,' says Hutton. Hutton first met Bob Brown in 1985, and they both soon realised they had similar aspirations to establish a national Green party. A group of 50 environmentalists had met in Tasmania in late December 1984 to begin planning a bigger national conference to work toward that end.

'We organised the "get together" conference in Sydney in 1986 with 600 delegates—it was a broad-based conference with people talking about all sorts of activist and environmental movements taking place at that time,' says Hutton. The Sydney conference was successful in getting a national coordination of environmental activists, but there were too many conflicting views to move forward with forming the Australian Greens.

'The conservation movement at the time was linking up with the Labor Party, with Graham Richardson as Environment minister and Phillip Toyne working at ACF [the Australian Conservation Foundation]. There was a feeling among the environment movement that there was more to be gained by sticking with the ALP,' says Hutton.

Moreover, the Democrats, whose votes were still on the increase federally, were arguing that they were the real Green party, says Hutton. On top of that, mirroring the split that had occurred within the German Greens Party, there was a more anarchistic faction who argued that politics was a dirty business, and they wanted no direct part in embracing it.

'Bob was dancing Green politics back then, but because his roots were so deep in the conservation movement he was very keen not to alienate the conservationists present. It was obvious to Bob and me that the only way for the Green party to go anywhere was to form a unified national party. We weren't going anywhere just forming one party here and another there; we needed to be a Green party in every share household in the country,' says Hutton.

It emerged that Queensland and Tasmania were closest in their visions for a strong national party, but the 1986 conference voted overwhelmingly against its establishment. Hutton later wrote that the conference demonstrated clearly to him and Brown how not to set up a Green party.

Brown later wrote in *The Greens*, the book he co-authored with Peter Singer, that 'it took six years to overcome that decision, but the delay was not entirely without benefits. It made it possible for The Greens to develop their own identity and differentiate themselves from the unstructured and vulnerable politics that had been so frustratingly obvious in Sydney in 1986.'

Drew Hutton travelled to Tasmania in July 1990 to see Bob Brown. He was able to report that in Queensland the Goss Labor Government had been elected and didn't have a strong environment platform. Meanwhile, federally Paul Keating had made his move for ALP leadership. Things weren't looking good for the environment. 'Bob and I looked at each other and agreed it was time for a Green party. The next twelve months was consulting with various groups and key people in the environment movement,' says Hutton.

In 1990, the Sydney Greens, who still held the registered name 'The Australian Greens', farmed out the national Greens registration to a number of state groups, creating deputy registry offices in each state. Drew Hutton became the registry officer in Queensland.

By 1991, a Green conference took place in Sydney attempting to bring together all the state register holders of the name the Greens. According to Hutton, the conference was fraught. 'It just blew up,' he says.

'The anti-party people were there, arguing that we shouldn't have an Australian Greens. Then there was the group led by Bob Brown and myself arguing for the Australian Greens—the unified national party. Then there was the Socialist Workers Party faction, particularly from New South Wales, arguing for no prescription of other parties. Nobody could agree on anything.'

How did Brown deal with that conflict? 'Brilliantly,' according to Hutton. 'He was pretty annoyed, but he kept arguing his point. He's pretty skilful in winning people over, although initially he didn't win people over in that context.' Brown and Hutton put their position, listened to others, and agreed to disagree.

Ben Oquist was also keeping a close eye on proceedings in Sydney, and says that the main problem was that people had their own agendas and allegiances to other organisations, rather than being simply committed to forming an Australian Green party. 'I think it needed to start a bit smaller with people who were actually committed to it, rather than trying to start with all these disparate groups,' he says.

'There were people with too much organisational baggage, so they were bringing their organisation to the table, rather than just their views . . . Bob and Drew wanted a national party, but all those other groups' allegiances weren't to

With dad Jack at Liffey, 1986.

Bringing home the horse, Liffey, 1980s. PHOTO BY JUDY HENDERSON.

With Peter Garrett, 'Save the Lemonthyme' rally, Cradle Mountain, 1987.

With Peter Garrett, Tully River, 1987.

'Save the Daintree' rally, Brisbane, 1987.

With Paul Thomas. PHOTO BY ROGER LOVELL.

With George Bush (senior), 1990. OFFICIAL WHITE HOUSE PHOTOGRAPH.

Tarkine, 1991. This campaign had an international impact and won the attention of the German media. PHOTO BY HUBERT.

Cloudy Bay, 1997. PHOTO BY PAUL THOMAS.

At Queen Mary Creek Falls, 1998. PHOTO BY PAUL THOMAS.

With the leader of the New Zealand Greens, Jeanette Fitzsimons, 1998.
PHOTO BY PAUL THOMAS.

With the Dalai Lama, Canberra, 2002.

Liffey.

forming a national party, they were first and foremost [loyal] to their own organisation. In the end it was left to people who were committed to a successful national Green organisation from the outset. There was no question in our minds of whether it was the way forward to form the Australian Greens, but those early get-togethers were still discussing whether it was a good idea.'

But by 1992, the New South Wales Greens had changed their position. Brown recalls: 'At a Friday night meal in a café in Newtown in Sydney, after some last-minute changes to the draft constitution, the New South Wales Greens representatives agreed to join with the Queensland and Tasmanian state Greens parties in forming a national identity.'

The New South Wales Greens recognised that the Socialist Workers Party (SWP), who already had their own political party, were holding back the progress of the Australian Greens. In a pivotal pragmatic move, it was agreed that members of the Greens couldn't simultaneously be members of other political parties, effectively trimming the divisive SWP element. Ben Oquist says it was one of the 'great, defining decisions' that allowed the national Greens party to come into existence.

'From those in the know,' says Oquist, 'that rule about not being in another party was just one of those great things that really helped us move forward. I'd seen how destructive the socialist element could be through other environmental organisations I'd been involved in. That's not to say you can't be a member of any other social group, just not another political party.'

The New South Wales Greens came on board with one concession—that they retain the power to mandate the policies of their candidates in parliament. The clause was written into the new Australian Greens constitution.

'What Bob and I were arguing for,' says Hutton, 'was a national organisation with strong local structures, and the states being fairly minimalist. What we got was a strong state and local structure, but a minimalist national one.' The Australian Greens became a confederation of states, rather than a unified national party.

The West Australian Greens were still a separate party altogether; Victoria and South Australia had little representation as yet. The WA Greens had been making inroads into the Australian Senate since 1984, when Jo Vallentine won a Senate seat representing the Nuclear Disarmament Party. She then represented the WA Greens in the Senate from 1990, becoming the first federally elected politician wearing the label 'Green', before Christabel Chamarette completed her parliamentary term from 1992. In 1994 Dee Margetts joined the Senate with the WA Greens (overlapping with Bob Brown's first Senate term).

'So,' explains Vallentine, 'for three years, there were two women Greens (WA) Senators simultaneously, and they created quite a stir over budget and procedure issues in the Senate because their votes were crucial. Prior to the formation of the Greens (WA), I had worked since 1984 on a gradually widening green agenda, starting with the single issue election on nuclear issues.'

Regardless of the WA Greens heading in their own parochial direction, the Australian Greens were now preparing candidates to run for the national elections. (At the National Greens conference in October 2003, the WA Greens finally announced that they would now officially become part of the unified Australian Greens.) Over the 1990s, Green parties from every other state came on board, with the Australian Capitol Territory and Victorian Greens forming in 1993, and Green parties forming in the Northern Territory and South Australia in 1995.

❧ ❧ ❧

The Australian Greens constitution was finalised and the ill-fated press conference called at the community centre in Lavender Bay, Sydney, on Sunday 30 August 1992.

'The media missed the moment,' says Hutton. 'Everybody knows Bob Brown now, but everyone didn't know Bob Brown then. Bob says anything now and it's covered; it wasn't the case back then. We still had a fair bit of trouble getting the media interested.'

Ben Oquist remembers the dispiriting press conference in Lavender Bay; he was the one who had organised it. 'There were no TV cameras, no mainstream newspapers. It's just that thing—if you don't exist, you don't exist. We said that we were a national party going places, but were we really? We didn't have any seats on the mainland. After that there were many things we did over the next years that nobody turned up to.'

Bob was determined to take his break from politics, and decided to support his lifelong friend Judy Henderson as the number one Greens Senate candidate from Tasmania for the 1993 federal election. Henderson says Bob was very tired after ten years in the Tasmanian Parliament. 'There was such a good team there in Tasmania, it wasn't all on his shoulders,' she says. 'There was a wonderful person to take up the Tasmanian leadership there in Christine Milne. Bob took a long while to decide whether or not he'd stand for the federal parliament. He was quite reluctant to do that, and then he finally decided he would run for [the Tasmanian federal lower house seat] Denison. He didn't have any illusions that he would get in. It was clearly very difficult. You always have that idea that maybe a miracle will happen and you might get in, but it was clearly always going to be very hard. It was making the break. It was the first time in Australia a Green had stood for the lower house. Somebody had to do it.'

'That was the time when the Australian Greens had just formed, and it was all about getting the profile. Bob is a supreme strategist; he is always looking at the long term, and how to push the movement along. He was interested in raising the profile of the Greens at that point, and certainly he did. A person with a public profile like his was the only way the Greens were going to get the sort of stature they needed,' said Henderson.

Brown stood for the federal lower house seat of Denison, well aware that he probably wouldn't be elected, but still wanting to give his ALP rival Duncan Kerr a good run for his money. In running for Denison, Brown was attempting to focus national attention on Hobart, where major environmental battles had been fought and won over the previous decade. He was also preparing the ground for the new confederation of Greens' entry into the national limelight. As the party's spokesperson, Brown was already becoming its flag-bearer. The identity would stick.

Standing down from his seat in the Tasmanian Parliament at the end of 1992, Brown handed the leadership of the Tasmanian Greens to Christine Milne. 'I don't believe in waiting until you know you're going to win a seat,' said Brown, 'that's never been my way of operating. We have to break through the barriers and not be led by opinion polls.' Former Tasmanian premier Michael Field had no doubt about Brown's agenda. 'Bob Brown has a very shrewd and sharp political mind,' he said. 'He knows he cannot win Denison, but the name of his game is to maximise the Green vote in the Senate. To do that he has to spearhead the Greens in an attempt on the lower house.'

It took some convincing for Brown to run for federal parliament. He had stated that he felt more effective as an activist for the many forest campaigns he had participated in over the previous years—Farmhouse Creek and the Picton forests in Tasmania, Coolangubra and Tantawangalo in New South Wales—than to feel locked away in Canberra. Brown had paid many visits to forest protest camps over the previous years, involving himself in direct action blockades on some occasions, and just offering encouraging words to tree-sitters and young protesters on others.

He says one of the things that tipped the balance in favour of pursuing national politics was the 'Doomsday Announcement' in December 1992. At the United Nations General Assembly, 1575 scientists from many nations, including 100 Nobel Prize winners, stated that the planet was in perilous danger of being uninhabitable within 30 to 40 years. 'We don't have time to be comfortable, to be relaxed,' said Brown. 'That really fired me into thinking again.'

He was to allude to the Doomsday Announcement some years later in his first speech to the Senate. 'They warned that if we do not change this material charge, this consumption of the planet, within 40 years life for many species, perhaps including our own, is likely to be unsustainable; that we are on a collision course with the planetary environment itself,' he said.

> Had that warning that the planet is going to collapse under the weight of human activities been a warning of a stock exchange collapse in this day and age of economic fundamentalism, it would have grabbed the front pages of the media around the planet. As it was, it missed most Australian newspapers. It made page nine of the Hobart *Mercury*, as I remember, and one of the mainland metropolitan dailies. Less space was given to that extraordinarily telling warning from a global scientific think-tank than to the 'Peanuts' cartoon of the same day around this country.

At the 1993 federal election, the issue was the GST. In two and half hours of live television debate between Liberal opposition leader John Hewson and then Prime Minister Paul Keating over three consecutive nights, the environment was not mentioned once.

Brown says that the Greens, the Democrats, and all other minor parties were 'squeezed out of the media limelight'. New ALP Environment minister Ros Kelly warned Brown that the Greens should acknowledge Labor's environmental achievements or risk losing credibility. Brown had championed the Greens' national election strategy, claiming there was little difference between the two major parties. 'I would like to remind Dr Brown,' said Kelly, 'that if Labor had not been in office for the past ten years, the Franklin River would have been dammed, the rainforests of the wet tropics would be stacked in a timber yard, and Kakadu would have been mined'.

Judy Henderson narrowly missed out—by just 1 per cent—on representing Tasmania in the Senate after a particularly nasty rumour aired in the Tasmanian press just two days before the election.

News circulated throughout the state that the Greens were responsible for a bomb being placed on a railway bridge near the town of Smithton in north-west Tasmania, with 'Earth First' written on a sheet beside it. State-wide blanket media coverage the day before the federal election decried 'eco-terrorism', and pointed the finger at the Greens. Christine Milne, who continues to raise the issue to the present day, says that the manoeuvre was a piece of direct election sabotage from the forestry industry, 'and it worked'. Milne points out that whoever wrote the sign even forgot to put the trademark exclamation mark at the end of the 'Earth First' slogan. (Earth First! is a radical US conservation group known for controversial action such as tree spiking. Their title is always cited with an exclamation mark after 'First'.)

Given the closeness of the result, if an anti-green group was behind the stunt, it may have made all the difference. Considering the history of lengths anti-green interests had gone to before in Tasmania, including election bribery and aeroplane sabotage, this kind of political sabotage doesn't seem unfeasible.

'The eco-terrorist event just happened in the last week, and we had been running very well in the polls,' recalls Henderson, who had the most to lose from the incident. 'If it was an election strategy against us, it was certainly very effective, just because it was going to be very tight anyway. That certainly contributed to pushing us down a rung.'

The new national Greens would have to wait until the 1996 federal election before they would enter the federal parliament, but they had made a significant impact in their federal electoral debut, helping to get Labor's Paul Keating over the line on preferences. But the Australian Greens failed to win a single federal seat.

Ben Oquist says it was a disappointing result for the Greens in their first year as a national party. The party had set up their first national office in Kings Cross in Sydney—a poky single room offered to the Greens by the editor of the magazine *Art Almanac*. 'It was tiny,' says Oquist. 'I remember I borrowed a little fan from a friend to put in there. That was a hard time. That '93 election was very polarised. If you were a progressive, you were against Hewson and voting with Keating. There was very little space for the Greens. We did expect to do better; we had high hopes. We thought we were offering a whole new set of ideals that weren't being offered by the Labor Party. But we just didn't get any airspace.'

However, the Greens gradually picked up voter interest throughout the mid-1990s, with Bob Brown lending his face to state campaigns all over the country. The party had early support in Victoria, with Andrea Sharam picking up 21 per cent in the Coburg by-election in May 1994, and then Peter Singer winning 28 per cent in Andrew Peacock's seat of Kooyong. Such results came in from Green candidates all over the country, including Australian Capital Territory Greens Kerrie Tucker and Lucy Horodny picking up the balance of power with independents in 1995 in the ACT Legislative Assembly.

Throughout the mid-1990s the divisions between the Greens and Democrats became more public and explicit. Brown had been talking with the Democrats leadership since the previous decade about the idea of forming the Green Democrats. Janet Powell, who led the Democrats, had been receptive to the idea and met with Tasmanian Green independents, including Brown, in 1991 to set the wheels in motion. However, when Cheryl Kernot took over the Democrats leadership in 1992, she had other ideas, and the merger was effectively derailed.

'The period with Janet Powell was very positive, there was a lot of serious thinking about it. But it was clear that the grass-roots of the Greens and the membership base of the Democrats were not happy about that at all,' recalls Judy Henderson. 'A lot of us, including Bob, did think it was ridiculous to have two progressive social justice, environmentally oriented parties, very close to one another, it seemed ridiculous not to form some sort of an alliance, or a merger. But there were a lot of territorial feelings against it.'

Bob continued campaigning for the Greens all over the country throughout the period of 1993–96, when he took his break from parliament. Judy Henderson, who still shared a house with Bob in Hobart, says it was a time of considerable financial hardship for Brown.

'Income was an issue around those years,' she says. 'People had told him that he would have no trouble getting on to the lecture circuit and that it would be an income-generating activity. In fact, that didn't happen. He had his name down on a few private organisations to link people up on such lecture circuits. But ... the time had passed for interest in such environmental speakers. Money has never been at the fore-front of Bob's mind. But it did get a bit tight at that time,' says Henderson.

Brown had planned to use the time out of parliament to turn his hand to serious environmental writing. For several years he had been talking about wanting to write his defini-tive environmental book on 'The Human Tragedy'. Bob had felt that the Tasmanian Parliament had come to restrict him in terms of his broader global green agenda. 'I think he was frustrated that he had to always focus on those local issues, and not do what he wanted to on the broader front,' says Henderson.

'He was always talking about writing this definitive book. He was always saying, "I must go up to Liffey and write".

People never allowed him, or he didn't allow himself the time. We all do it—keep putting things off and allow ourselves to be snared by any number of things,' she said.

Brown continued in his role as Greens national spokesperson, and collaborated with ethicist Peter Singer to write the book *The Greens*. The book outlined what the authors saw as the major crisis facing the planet, and put forward a vision for a future in which green politics would come to the fore. It also traced the difficulties the Greens had faced in their early years in Tasmania and nationally, and presented the Greens' policy on issues ranging from environmental taxes to drugs policy, from health and education to growth and employment.

Some of the book's more controversial policy positions included environmental tax hikes for business and industry, a guaranteed adequate income for all, and legalising heroin and marijuana—a policy they would be pilloried for in the New South Wales state election six years later with headlines in the tabloid press such as 'Ecstasy over the counter: Greens' hidden drug policy revealed'. The Greens also supported a moratorium on new freeways, and strict regulation on foreign investment into Australia.

Ben Oquist says that for young Greens enthusiasts such as himself, the book by Brown and Singer was tremendously important.

'No-one knew what we were about before that. At least the book helped to show we did exist and stood for something. It wasn't a perfect book by any means and it's easy to look back on it critically. But at the time, it was fantastic to have a book out like that. I was desperate to read half a sentence about the Greens, let alone a whole book . . . That was a time when we didn't have any media anywhere—none. So even one step like that was very important to us,' says Oquist.

Although the book provided a neat template for the Greens party members themselves, it didn't have a huge impact on the national debate. It wasn't the definitive text that Bob had wanted for many years to write. The book was released to coincide with the 1996 federal election, and in some cases became fodder for political commentators to attack the party. The Greens' policies were also attacked on the grounds that many of the policies outlined in the book weren't costed.

In the week leading up to the election, Sydney Institute Executive Director Gerard Henderson wrote in the *Sydney Morning Herald* under the headline 'Major parties should shun the Greens' that Brown and Singer's book 'sounds like the remnants of the socialist left having a whinge . . . until you realise that it also sounds like sections of the conservative right'. Henderson compared the book to the writings of Australian conservative political commentator and Roman Catholic layman Bob Santamaria in regard to its 'apocalyptic messages providing evidence of a crisis mentality at work'.

Comparisons between the Greens and religious movements would continue. It seemed to be the only way that the media was able to classify and compartmentalise the party.

The divisions between the Greens and Democrats would become increasingly bitter in the weeks leading up to the 1996 election, as they both recognised that their relative ascendancy increasingly depended on the other's relative demise.

This tussle played itself out most vociferously in Tasmania where Brown's Senate election largely depended on the Democrats' Robert Bell being ousted. In October 1995, Brown was wording up the media about the aspirations of the Greens. 'We are not a preference machine, we are not a ginger group, we are not a lobby group. The Greens are in this to take power,' he said in the *Age*. He added that a merger with the Democrats was still 'inevitable'.

Democrats leader Cheryl Kernot, for her part, repeatedly rejected the notion of a merger, describing the Greens as 'anarchistic' and having 'a blinkered view on the world'. Her strategy with the Democrats was to move closer to the major parties in policy positions, and thus have more of a direct input in the parliament. Tasmanian Democrats Senator Bell was also upping the ante, describing Brown in the week before the election as a caricature of himself, 'prancing' about the country and spending little time in Tasmania. Brown renounced Bell for preferencing to Reverend Fred Nile's Call to Australia Party.

The two parties were clearly coming from different poles, as Brown noted a week before the election when he described the Democrats as 'weak and second class' for their policy of never blocking supply to the government of the day. 'They [had] made themselves the weaker senators of the future' in his judgment.

Ben Oquist was the Greens' national media coordinator leading up to the 1996 election, and he recalls the negative media coverage the party started receiving. However, it was a positive step that the party was receiving coverage at all, says Oquist, and the issue of the sale of Telstra was the first time journalists came looking for comment from Bob Brown on a non-environmental issue.

'We did finally get a little bit of traction in the media, mainly over the Telstra sale. We just had a little bit of relevance there because people knew we had a good chance of getting into the Senate, and may have an impact on that issue,' he says.

As it became clearer that Brown was about to win his Senate seat, the media campaign against the Greens switched into top gear. The financial press was also doing its bit to try to warn voters off the Greens prior to the election. On 19 February *Business Review Weekly* ran with a cover story under the headline 'The Green Menace'. The article's author David Forham described Brown as a master of political brinkmanship, and said:

> the exasperation of political parties in their relationship with the Greens flows largely from an inability to classify them in any framework that can be understood in usual political terms. The Greens do not see the environment in isolation, but as the foundation for a vision of global revolution. Brown is an evangelist for the environment and

practises a fundamentalist brand of politics. He believes that he and the Green movement are there to literally save the world. This means compromise is out of the question.

Unnamed major-party MPs were quoted in the article, talking about the Greens' inconsistency. 'Another senior minister says the position of the Greens might be as easily explained by the phases of the moon [and] cosmic movements as by political philosophy, judging by the lack of a pattern to their voting habits . . . Another minister describes them as anarchists.'

The policies that Brown was bringing to Canberra were 'chilling' from a business point of view, claimed Forham, such as the Greens' aim to 'seek a greater level of accountability and affiliation by businesses to the communities they serve'. Chilling stuff indeed.

The anti-Greens position would continue to be articulated in the years ahead, incremental with the party's swelling popularity, and delivered with increasing zeal. Brown had won his Senate seat at the expense of Tasmanian Democrats Senator Robert Bell. He joined West Australian Greens Senator Dee Margetts in the federal parliament, following Christabel Chamarette's loss to Democrat Andrew Murray.

As the first Australian Greens representative in the federal parliament, Brown had a formidable challenge in front of him—to hold the newly formed party's flag securely aloft, and operate as a sole environmental agent of change in the federal Senate. Nonetheless, he had enough experience under his belt from the divided and frequently murky realm of Tasmanian politics to confidently embrace the challenge at hand.

'It was very important to have him there at that stage,' says Drew Hutton. 'I don't want to overstate Bob's importance, but it's also possible to understate it. The mid to late '90s were a very difficult period for the party. There would have still been a Green party established at that stage without Bob. But he gave the party its momentum; he was one of many very important people maintaining that energy. He just worked so hard.'

❧ ❧ ❧

With the Senate seat secured, Bob Brown was still president and founding patron of the Australian Bush Heritage Fund. But he knew he would have to shake off the role before he entered federal parliament.

Doug Humann, current Bush Heritage Fund CEO, says that the organisation has gone from strength to strength since its establishment in 1990. However, by late 1996, with a board of ten and a staff of three part-timers, there was a glaring need for it to professionalise. Bob Brown stepped down as president in January 1997, just as Humann became CEO.

'In late 1996, Bob saw that the Fund had a fantastic future,' says Humann. 'It had by that stage bought properties in Tasmania, Western Australia, Queensland and New South Wales. I think he felt that his continued role as president was going to inhibit the organisation from prospering as he imagined it should. He knew that people would see him as the leader, and thus wouldn't support the organisation. He thought it had a broader opportunity to gather a very diverse range of Australians to support it financially without him as president.'

Humann today travels all over Australia gathering financial supporters for the organisation from the corporate sector. He says he is often greeted with an initial negativity when business people realise Bob Brown's close involvement.

'I now spend a lot of time with wealthy Australians, corporate types, often in Sydney and Melbourne,' he says. 'It's interesting to hear and see their reactions when they realise Bob's involvement with the organisation. Bob remains our founding patron, as is pointed out in all our annual reports. It's probably not surprising that people react to Bob because of what they perceive as his extremism.'

'When I explain the story that Bush Heritage was only established because of Bob's generosity and altruism, including the Goldman Prize money in 1990 to start the ball rolling, there is an immediate switch in attitude and understanding of Bob. It's been quite astounding. Quite a few business people, when I first walk in the door, the hackles have been up, but when I tell the story, they are astonished that somebody could be that altruistic, as to give away that amount of money. The turnaround in their perception of Bob is absolutely immediate,' says Humann.

The concept of the Australian Bush Heritage Fund is not an original one. Similar organisations already had been established in Canada, the US and Europe when it was founded. However, the idea of buying back the bush has won many supporters in Australia. The growth of the organisation coincided with a time in Australia's environmental history when the environment was being pushed off the agenda of the federal government, as Paul Keating and John Howard retreated from making significant new additions to national parks and conservation areas throughout the 1990s to the present day.

'Bob recognised that this would be a very effective way to protect those wonderful wild places,' says Humann. 'That's why we've been able to get such strong support from the corporate sector; it's so direct and tangible. People give us money, we buy land and look after it forever. That was the dream that Bob had, and that's what we're doing.'

Humann says that in the early days of the organisation the priority was to buy small, strategically placed properties designed to raise the Bush Heritage profile. 'By contrast [in] November 2003 [we] bought a 214 000-hectare property in Queensland named Ethabuka Station. There's no question that without Bob's early involvement in forming the organisation, we wouldn't be where we are now.'

The Australian Bush Heritage Fund has now acquired close to a million acres of bushland around Australia. Since its financially difficult beginning, the organisation today turns a profit and continues to generate financial supporters from all over Australia.

'I guess Bob tends to be campaigning on immediate issues at hand, and thus he is not as well known for this. But I'm pretty sure he would regard this organisation as one of the most significant things he has been a part of. He certainly holds it very close to his heart, though with no sense of proprietorialism or ownership . . . It was an idea whose time had come, and Bob was the one to make the idea a reality,' says Humann.

Having stepped aside from the Bush Heritage Fund, Brown embarked on the formidable task of leading Australia's newest political party in the federal parliament. Ben Oquist says he suspects the Australian Greens may not have survived as a party had Brown not secured his place in the federal Senate in 1996.

'I'm not sure the Greens would have been able to get off the ground at all. Having somebody in the parliament that you can organise around, that gives you a national profile, a vital bit of political capital you can move to other states . . . I remember thinking at that time, when the count was on and it was close—what would we have done if he didn't get in? We were thinking, it was the second time he'd run . . . If the electorate rejects you twice, you start to think about what to do.'

'I still think to this day that the Greens might not have made it without him winning that election. Now, of course, he's as Tasmanian as the Tasmanian tiger, I can no longer see him separated from it,' says Oquist.

International Chapter 12
Green perspectives

Having successfully made the transition from state to federal politics, Bob Brown was also honing his international political awareness and focus.

Throughout his time in the Tasmanian Parliament in the 1980s, Brown became increasingly frustrated by the narrow scope of the parliamentary work he was able to engage with as a Tasmanian MP. Throughout the Franklin campaign Brown was given an international voice, albeit a fleeting one, quoted in media reports as far afield as Russia, Japan and across Europe. Brown knew that in order to achieve this access to an international audience again, he needed to penetrate the Australian national parliament.

Ironically, Brown exemplifies the notion that working from a peripheral political footing can be a very empowering motivator. 'In cities, people often feel like they're in an anonymous sea of people in which they feel disempowered,' he says. 'Whereas when you're on the edge and you've got a mountain at the back reminding you of the wilderness, and you've got log trucks constantly rolling down the street, it does confront you. It helps you to realise you do have the power to change things.'

Ben Oquist says that Bob Brown is someone 'who is always looking outwards'. 'He's not just thinking about Tasmania, he's thinking about Australia. And beyond Australia, he's always thinking globally. He is always looking one step, bigger picture than where you're at right now . . . That's one of the great things about working for him, he's always got one more ambitious issue up his sleeve.'

Oquist says Bob Brown is interested in leading by example. 'He says the internationalisation of the Greens is not going to happen from Europe or the States, there are too many people there looking inward and thinking they are at the centre. It is going to happen from a peripheral place like Australia.'

Brown's globalisation vision begins with global democracy, and sets the environment as the key issue from which all economic considerations should spring forth. 'The Greens haven't come close to our global potential by a long shot, but it is terribly important that we do,' says Brown.

'There is a defacto world governance by the multinational corporations these days, and it's backed up by the Bush admin-istration and other governments. The only way we'll get out of this age of wealth based on resource extraction is to have an equally potent global alternative, and it's got to be a demo-cratic one.'

If the Greens are going to grow with the same kind of reach as multinational corporations, Brown believes the party needs to establish equally strong global connections. He has frequently put his vision for global democratic governance, based on the model of 'one person, one vote, one value'. This 'democrati-cally based globalisation', said Brown in a recent speech at the Sydney Institute, will be 'much healthier, safer and fairer than the market-based globalisation we have now. The rewards will be enormous in economic and employment terms but spread much more democratically for the world's citizens.'

This vision puts Brown at variance with some Greens, who favour the view that the party should always embrace a localised focus—the view that Greens are more effective when fostering local community connections and prioritising local governance. 'I see that we're in an age of globalised human community, mass communications have ensured that, and mass travel. We have to be able to have that administered in the best way, through democracy, that is possible,' says Brown. 'That does require such things as some form of democratic input from people about how world trade should be regulated. About whether the nuclear industry, including the nuclear weapons industry, is a valid one in an age where there is so much poverty.'

Brown predicts it is inevitable that there will be a new model of global democracy in the future, but that the biggest opposition to it will come from the US administration, 'people who tout democracy morning, noon and night—but really don't mean it,' he says.

The Green Party in its many international guises, is one of the first internationally networked political parties that has aspirations for global political power and influence. Bob Brown has been one of its most vociferous advocates. As much as the environment is an issue that crosses international borders, particularly in regard to issues such as depletion of the ozone layer, global warming, the extinction of species and deforestation, Green parties have arisen globally to meet that calling.

There are now Green parties in every continent of the globe, although the various parties' aspirations and political footing are at great variance. In broad terms, we can say that the most politically successful Green parties are presently in Europe, notably Germany, while the Greens have not yet made a significant dent on the US political landscape. In Australia, we are currently watching the party's ascendancy.

Bob Brown had forged many contacts with Greens all over the world, and had been one of the key proponents of the concept of 'green' or 'positive' globalisation.

Prior to the turn of the millennium, the concept of a global Greens party was purely academic. There was contact between Greens on a personal level—most notably between Bob Brown and other leading international Greens such as Petra Kelly and Ralph Nader (both of whom have visited Bob's place in Liffey) but the party had failed to formalise its international links.

Since 1997, members of the newly formed Australian Greens started talking up the idea of having a Global Greens conference in Australia. After four years of intensive organising, the Global Greens conference in Canberra in 2001 became the biggest convergence of international Green delegates ever assembled, bringing together over 800 delegates from 70 countries, representing every continent.

In opening the conference, Bob Brown articulated some of the core values that he perceived Greens from all over the world share. 'Since the collapse of communism, materialism or economic rationalism—the rule of money over values—has had full rein. Materialism's failure to consider the long-term consequences of its social and environmental exploitation has stolen hope from ordinary lives, leading to rising rates of cynicism, drug abuse, and suicide among young people, not least in the richest nations of Earth.'

'We Greens are the balancing factor, the natural reaction to this divisive ideology from the big end of town. Where they value shares, we share values,' Brown told the conference.

Conference convener Margaret Blakers says that over a period of four years organising the Global Greens conference, one of the biggest challenges was locating and contacting Greens groupings all over the world. 'Simply getting 800 people from 70 different countries was quite an amazing feat. When you walked into that place—it was just palpable—the air of expectation, that history was happening right here in front of our eyes . . . despite all the differences there was this sense that we all had a common agenda. People were bursting into tears—it was emotionally completely overwhelming. We sat until all hours of the night working out the charter. It wasn't a perfect process, but it was a process. People working and reworking clauses, sending them back to subgroups, and eventually taking them back to the floor. Getting all those different delegates and all those countries to agree on a charter was just incredible,' said Blakers.

As well as drafting the new Global Greens Charter the conference also ratified a 'Global Greens Coordination and Network'. Key elements of this document include the aim to 'foster and focus communications and actions among its members so that members of all Green political parties of the planet, on a continuing basis, will share knowledge of Green Party affairs and initiatives on issues of global concern'.

Furthermore, three delegates were elected to coordinate the ongoing communication, which would primarily be conducted via email. It was agreed that a primary focus of the coordination was to identify possible global actions to be proposed to the parties worldwide and to assist every Green party to access the relevant communications technologies.

In short, the broad aim of the Global Green network was to 'develop healthy discussion [among global Greens], especially via electronic mechanisms'. The charter marks an important moment in the formation of the Global Green movement— moving it from the academic to the actual by directly engaging with the technological mechanisms to bring a truly global green decision-making capacity into place.

There were some issues aired at the conference that clearly illustrated substantial differences between the individual Green parties assembled.

To some African delegates, for example, the issue of gay law reform was highly controversial. Questions about whether to work toward reforming or abolishing international economic bodies such as the International Monetary Fund (IMF) and World Bank also divided the party floor. Most European Greens favoured the abolition option, while other representatives were more in favour of reforming the institutions through incorporating notions of environmental sustainability and environmental accountability.

Moreover, it has become clear since the conference that one of the key problems facing the global Green vision is the task of ongoing international Greens coordination. This issue has yet to be resolved. Blakers says: 'The Global Green movement is still at toddler stage—all the mechanisms are there, but it is still somewhat reactive.'

'The problem in the west is that the electoral system locks the Greens out of government. I think the Greens will strengthen and develop a proactive capacity to act with a global reach. The level to use communications technologies is strengthening all the time among Greens. We will get resources, we will get think tanks, be able to videoconference internationally. We are the only global political movement and we will build on that. It's an environmental crisis coinciding with a communications revolution—it's a globalisation issue—we present the opposite to corporate globalisation. If we don't have political movements that are global, we leave the field to the corporations.'

Brown says he sees human failings as the main barriers to the Greens reaching their global potential. 'People are absolutely attracted to, and put their mental energies into what is happening in their direct field of view—we all do it. But the multinationals are planning in their boardrooms how to link up their global operations. We don't tend to do that, and even when we do, it's hard to get the attention of someone else who's fighting the latest election campaign in their own country.'

❧ ❧ ❧

Global Greens media statements and press releases are circulated throughout the world, amended and commented on, and eventually released to the global media. If the Greens are able to finetune this global reach, they will increasingly become a force to be reckoned with in the new millennium.

'It does take a lot of people taking a breath and lifting their head out of the sand—all of us—to change that,' says Brown.

At a time when Australia is gaining more of an international standing than ever before on the global radar, Bob Brown has also developed a growing international notoriety. He is frequently interviewed by major international news agencies such as CNN, often called on to articulate the counterpoint to Australian Government positions.

There is a growing international demand for politicians able to articulate sound alternative perspectives. An increasingly alarming international environmental crisis has occurred simultaneously with a revolution in information technologies— pushing the Global Green movement closer together with the imperative to act, coupled with the technological means to coordinate.

The Greens have joined other activist movements (such as anti-war and anti-globalisation demonstrators) in becoming the proponents of a new grassroots, ethically founded form of globalisation.

The most significant western protest movement of the 1990s was undoubtedly the anti-globalisation protests that met global delegates at IMF, World Bank and other economic forums in North America, Europe and Australia. When the World Economic Forum came to Melbourne on 11 September, 2000, the city was brought to a standstill as thousands of protesters converged on the Crown Casino. Bob Brown joined the protesters outside, telling them, 'Those representatives from the top end of town would do well to listen to these people on the streets. It's like the mobilisation of the masses, surrounding the tower of the elite.'

The Greens globally have emerged as the party closest to being able to take those waves of demonstrations into the parliaments of the world. If the Greens act fast, they are in a position to capitalise on this, and could pick up the collective anger of the anti-globalisation generation, many of whom can now be identified as part of generation X or Y, young people between the ages of 22 and 36.

Ben Oquist says he has witnessed many of those former anti-globalisation protesters coming to the Greens. 'I think before the Greens, those anti-globalisation people would have just said no to politics full stop. But now, come election time, a lot of those people are active for the Greens.'

The Greens still pick up the votes of the disaffected. As Petra Kelly frequently stated throughout the 1980s and early 1990s, the Greens are perceived as the 'anti-party party', and this gives them exclusive credibility in the minds of the current crop of globalisation and anti-war demonstrators. The Greens are viewed as having ethical credibility, even in the minds of an increasingly cynical generation.

Bob Brown has set himself the task of being an independent agent of international aid on a number of occasions. On 23 February 2002, Rebels of the Revolutionary Armed Forces (FARC) kidnapped Ingrid Betancourt, Greens candidate for Colombian presidency, when she and her entourage drove into rebel-controlled territory. On 4 May 2002 Bob Brown, flanked by bodyguards, against Australian Government advice, led a street-leafleting campaign in downtown Bogotá with other Greens, holding a life-sized cardboard cutout photo of the missing Colombian presidential candidate. Betancourt is still being held captive.

In July 1999 Brown made a secret mission to Tibet in order to see for himself the treatment of the Tibetans under militarised Chinese rule. Brown's visit came at a time when the Howard Government was reopening political dialogues with China. After his trip, Brown called on the Australian Government to scrap the controversial dialogue because of the clear evidence he had seen there of extensive, military repression of Tibetan culture.

However, these trips were largely self-motivated undertakings that do not necessarily provide evidence of the Greens functioning as a global political force. Ben Oquist says he considers the Greens' claim to be the first globally networked political party as 'a claim waiting to be fulfilled'.

'We are globally networked, but not very well networked. It's amazing, though, when you go around to the Greens offices all over the planet . . . the similarities are striking. They have the same kinds of people involved, relating in the same kinds of ways. It's not as though there's all these parties which are totally different with the same name. I think it is a genuine global reaction to the same thing—to economic rationalism, to the destruction of the planet . . . that kind of resistance to all the negatives that are occurring . . . We do see ourselves as the positive form of globalisation. People like to describe those activists as anti-everything, but they're not, they actually want to do something positive . . .

'Capital is transnational, governments work transnationally. If we are going to beat them, we're going to have to do it on a transnational scale. I don't think we are yet, not consistently. It's a bit like the Australian Greens were ten years ago—all these little pockets around Australia. Yes, we all believed in the same things, yes, there was this connection between us all. But you'd hardly know it. It wasn't consolidated.'

The September 11 attacks on New York and the Pentagon undoubtedly ushered in a period of deep questioning for the left. For many, the target had previously been the USA; the American brand of consumerism and free market capitalism that seemed to be homogenising the planet into a destructive grab that blighted the world's environment. But here was a situation beyond the politics of left and right—America, and particularly Americans themselves, deserved sympathy for the damage inflicted on the World Trade Centre.

Many believed that this political realignment would seriously diminish the Green vote. In fact, as Ben Oquist explains, the opposite happened. 'After the September 11 attacks there was a lot of speculation that the Greens would lose our votes, that we would lose our momentum along with the anti-globalisation movement.'

'We endorsed the Melbourne S11 [anti-globalisation] protest before it happened, which felt like quite a radical action to some, endorsing this mass civil disobedience without really knowing where it was going to go. People said the same about Bali, no-one will vote Green in this climate. Then we had our best ever result in the 2001 election and won Cunningham right after the Bali attack.'

The Green vote, and the personal popularity of Bob Brown, seems sufficiently solid to endure a rapidly shifting international political landscape. However, the Greens internationally need to coordinate a lot more effectively if they hope to tap their potential to become a global, proactive and politically powerful force across the world in the new millennium.

While Bob Brown brought forward a vision for the internationalisation of the Greens, it will take a new generation of Greens members to push for that vision to become a reality through engagement with information technologies. Bob Brown himself is not a technology enthusiast. 'He doesn't know how to use the internet or email,' says Ben Oquist. 'For Bob it's a waste of time. Bob's work and writing time is so precious, it's now better to sit Bob down with a pen and paper and get him to write something. He took to mobile phones really well, that was such a Bob technology.'

These are technologies the party will have to utilise in a more effective manner before the vision of a strong global Greens party coming to the fore in this century will even begin to manifest.

Despite his lack of personal proficiency in some of the new technologies, Bob Brown is well aware of their revolutionary potential. 'Just when the big end of town thought the miracle of the internet was for business it turns out that it is bigger still for people power,' Brown said after the 2003 anti-war protests. 'The internet cuts the rug from under Murdoch-style censorship, and connects the people being attacked with those sent to do the attacking. In a startling way this high tech is empowering people and enhancing our common humanity.

It has been a key to these huge rallies against the Iraq War being organised.'

Brown believes the Greens support will keep flooding in globally as a result of a perception that major parties with roots in social justice movements are simply being viewed as no longer socially just. It is a trend that holds across the board—from the Australian Labor and British Labour Party, to the American Democrats, and many other major parties the world over. This is where the Greens can take up the gauntlet.

'Even the German Green coalition is very different to a Green government with an ecological perspective underpinning every policy decision,' Brown says. 'In Schroeder's government, same as with the Green–ALP accord in Tasmania, we're caught in the position of greening up a little the market fundamentalism of a Labor Party. That's not where we need to be. We need to implement a Green policy platform—which is very different to the Labor Party, in fact more different than the difference between them and the Liberals.'

'That's where the Greens are the only new global political movement in the world in the twenty-first century,' declares Brown. 'If we drop the baton somebody else will take it up. I just think it's absolutely inevitable that there will be a popular movement to oppose market fundamentalism and extreme capitalism, that division we have between wealthy and poor people now. If the Greens don't succeed in doing that, someone else will, but the times will be more dire. That's the real question—is the world going to move on through intelligence or catastrophe?'

Into Chapter 13
the Senate

'The future will either be green or not at all.'

This dramatic quote from British philosopher, Jonathon Porritt began Bob Brown's maiden speech to the Australian Senate at 5.15 p.m. on 10 September 1996. He was speaking as the first ever member of the Australian Greens to address federal parliament's upper house and it would have seemed likely that his radical words would grab the attention of the Australian media.

However, at the time Brown delivered his maiden speech, the Australian Greens Party was not taken seriously by the mainstream media. The media had a much more meaty and sensational target—Pauline Hanson. At the very same time Hanson was delivering her maiden speech in the House of Representatives—minute to minute—Bob Brown was delivering his maiden speech in the Senate.

Yet the media failed to report one word of Brown's speech, while Hanson's became front-page news all over the country. In fact, some people in the Senate were listening to Hanson's speech on their headphones as Bob Brown was giving his speech.

'Normally a maiden speech would attract some interest, even just a line,' says Ben Oquist. 'But the whole press gallery was just transfixed by Hanson. They were utterly galvanised by it. Bob's speech didn't get a mention. It was a bit like that Lavender Bay press conference, all that nervous energy, and no-one covered it. But Bob was a much better person after giving that speech, and a much-changed person.'

At the same time that Bob was frankly articulating the broad sweep of Green aspirations for social change he was also rearranging his personal life, embarking on the committed relationship with Paul Thomas that endures to this day.

The pair purchased a small, well-positioned house in Mount Nelson on the picturesque hilly outskirts of Hobart, with a nature reserve out the back. They quickly settled into a domestic routine that would provide stability and respite for each.

They regularly feed the possums and have barbeques on the back porch. Bob's old piano sits in the foyer. The staple meal in Paul and Bob's place (at least when Bob is cooking) is steak and three veg. The fridge is affixed with all manner of invitations and placards for political and social functions. The dining room table is an ocean of paper, the place where Bob does his writing these days, when he finds the time.

It is an orderly, comfortable and well-domesticated professional life. Paul Thomas and Bob Brown enjoy in their Mt Nelson house. Bob doesn't get out to Liffey very much these days either, although the house is still there, with its trespassers welcome sign out the front. Since 1996 his anchor has shifted from Liffey to Paul.

Bob spends most of his time living between the house with Paul in Mount Nelson and various hotel rooms in Canberra.

And although Canberra can get tiresome, Bob speaks with Paul at least once a day when he's away, and says, 'Look, anyone who complains too much about the lifestyle of being in Canberra shouldn't be there in the first place'.

❧ ❧ ❧

For Bob Brown and the newly formed Greens, the early years in Parliament House in Canberra were slow and difficult.

One of the first issues Brown was called into the media spotlight over was the privatisation of Telstra. In order to get the Telstra bill through the Senate the Howard Government needed to win the support of either the Greens or independents. Just weeks prior to entering the parliament, Brown told reporters that he had spoken to Communications Minister Senator Robert Hill. 'I've made it clear to the senator that the sale of Telstra is not on as far as the Australian Greens are concerned because it will lead to an enormous loss of revenue to the Government, which has to be made up by cutting services or increasing taxes,' said Brown.

It wouldn't be his last word on the sale of Telstra, as later political machinations would bear out. But it was the first time the national media had come to the Greens seeking comment on an issue other than the environment.

By June 1997, Brown was back in the news, having been arrested during a logging blockade in the East Gippsland forests in Victoria. Brown, along with six other protesters, was charged with obstructing a forest operation in the Goolengook forests, north-east of Orbost. The protesters were voicing their opposition to the state and federal government having signed the controversial Regional Forest Agreement (RFA), which Brown described as a 'sham, a licence to log wild forests'.

Brown later commented that if Prime Minister Howard and Victorian Premier Jeff Kennett were serious about the environment, they should be the ones getting arrested. 'With such contentious forests, it shouldn't be me, it should be John Howard and Jeff Kennett who are standing down there in the forests. But instead of that, they're giving the forests the death warrant ... the protesters are down there doing their job for them.'

In August 1997, Brown caused a fracas when he put a motion to the Senate procedures committee to abandon the mandatory prayer reading (including the Lord's Prayer) at each sitting of the house. Brown suggested that it should be replaced with 'an invitation to prayer and reflection'. He said it would be an opportunity for senators to reflect on their responsibilities, rather than being forced into Christian worship. Brown commented that the prayers were 'only relevant to people who like an antiquated language'.

Catholic Archbishop Francis Carroll angrily responded that the motion would mean senators would cease to 'acknowledge a power higher than themselves'.

Meanwhile, the Australian Bush Heritage Fund continued to grow, and by the end of 1997 had announced its seventh property acquisition—120 hectares of unprotected coastal heathland between the Freycinet and Friendly Beaches national parks on Tasmania's east coast. The Bush Heritage Fund, which by this stage boasted 4000 financial supporters around Australia pouring in $750 000 per year, purchased the botanically diverse land for $253 650.

By May 1998 Brown made an impassioned plea to the parliament to pass sex discrimination legislation that would give equal rights to homosexuals in regard to superannuation, property law and will entitlement. Brown told the parliament that as a gay man he had suffered verbal abuse and threats of violence on numerous occasions. He spoke of one recent occasion in Hobart where he had been assailed by a man who 'with all the worst epithets that can be put against people on the basis of sexuality, threatened to punch me and threatened to beat me up'.

'We have to find a means of making sure that expressions of their own sexuality are not trammelled by discrimination which can be ugly, destructive, punitive, financially penalising,' he said.

Meanwhile in Queensland the One Nation Party was rising to prominence, with its leader Pauline Hanson having been elected to the federal parliament a couple of years earlier. One Nation had risen from nowhere on a far right populist platform of xenophobia and intolerance, and the party was gaining significant voter support. In the crucial Queensland election campaign in mid-1998 which saw One Nation at their peak, the Greens made it clear they would be doing all in their power to stop One Nation. The Greens put One Nation last in all 46 seats for the Queensland election. Brown recognised that the election was likely to be a close call, and that Green preferences would be crucial in locking out One Nation and giving the ALP a hefty chance of throwing out the Liberals. 'The Greens have been active in campaigning against One Nation and campaigning for the environment, recently organising nationwide peaceful protests urging voters to put the One Nation Party last,' said Brown.

Despite winning substantial voter support in Queensland that year, One Nation failed to come close to winning any significant political footing, and ALP Premier Peter Beattie was elevated to power.

By the end of the 1990s, the environment was starting to edge its way back onto the national agenda, partly bolstered by conservative environmental support from groups such as Doctors for Forests that sprang up all over the country. Support for the Greens was growing, and they were now regularly out-polling the Democrats. The WA Greens won five seats and the balance of power in the West Australian upper house in 2001, and the Greens out-polled the Democrats in Queensland and the Ryan by-election for the Queensland federal seat of Ryan that same year.

However, out of the rise of One Nation, a new political bottom line had been established. One of the policy directions that John Howard inherited from One Nation was a tougher line on border protection, and the introduction of the temporary protection visa (TPV). This meant that the government could determine which refugees constituted genuine asylum seekers, and which were 'queue jumpers'. Queue jumpers would be granted TPVs and locked up in desert camps, often for years. Kim Beazley stated that the ALP were fairly much in agreement with the Coalition's tough line to deter refugees from entering Australia by greeting those that did arrive with the most severe reception.

Labor had always been very strong advocates of border protection, with Gough Whitlam saying that he was 'not having hundreds of fucking Vietnamese Balts coming into the country' in response to the first arrivals of Vietnamese boat people in 1975.

Clearly, there was a massive 'middle ground' for the Greens to step into.

❧ ❧ ❧

Adopting a more compassionate stand in regard to refugees, the Greens picked up on a rising tide of popular opposition from both sides of politics. Many former ALP and even Coalition members now firmly believed that Australia's border protection policies had gone too far, and were a shameful and cold-hearted indictment on the entire country.

The Greens' softer line on refugees led some to claim that Bob Brown had become the 'conscience of the nation'. This perception first emerged during the debates over mandatory sentencing that had swept the country throughout 2000, in which Bob Brown had become one of the most consistent and outspoken opponents. The issue captured the nation's attention when it was reported that Aboriginal teenagers in the Northern Territory, some as young as twelve, were being sentenced to detention centres for extraordinarily trivial crimes.

There was the seventeen-year-old Aboriginal boy Johnno, from Groote Eylandt, who hanged himself in Darwin's Don Dale Detention Centre in February 2000, after being sentenced to 90 days for stealing textas and liquid paper. This case captured the attention and heart felt emotion of the nation, but there were many others.

The Northern Territory Greens first notified the federal Greens as early as 1998 of the appalling reality that children were being sentenced to gaol terms in the Northern Territory because of these laws. Bob Brown made it a federal policy priority, spearheading a massive campaign in the southern states of Australia, speaking at street demonstrations in Melbourne and Sydney. The Greens introduced legislation via a private member's bill in the Senate to repeal the laws.

'Finally we got those laws through the Senate—it was the only private member's bill to get through the Senate in my whole time there,' recalls Ben Oquist. 'There have only ever been three private member's bills passed. In the end Howard got Dennis Bourke [the then Northern Territory Chief Minister] to tone down the laws.'

It was significant that at that time Prime Minister Howard had an almost armour-plated reputation—he seemed to be almost above reproach within his own party. On this occasion however, there were eight Liberals threatening to cross the floor in the House of Representatives over the mandatory sentencing issue. Media pressure was also significantly swayed against the Northern Territory laws.

'To my mind, it was . . . mandatory sentencing that really brought Bob to prominence for the first time on a national issue that had nothing to do with the environment. It raised so many issues—how we treat our Indigenous people in Australia specifically. It was the time when he first came to be viewed as the conscience of the nation,' says Oquist.

By the time of the *Tampa* incident in August 2001, there was already a considerable undercurrent of dissent brewing over Australia's hardline immigration position. What ensued was a situation where the Australian Government did all within its power (regardless of international shipping laws) to prevent the *Tampa* from even arriving on Australian shores. When that failed, an incident that has come to be known as the 'children overboard' affair saw the government use misleading images of the refugees throwing their children over the side of the boat in an apparent effort to garner sympathy from the Australian people.

When the Howard Government's accusations were proven to be baseless, there was a nasty aftertaste left from the incident. But at the time, with an election close, the incident provided Howard with a chance to outmanoeuvre both the ALP and One Nation. This way, Howard could demonstrate that the ALP didn't have a strong position on border protection that differed from the government's (Beazley stated in the parliament that 'we support the government's actions in regard to the motor vessel *Tampa*'), and also win back those voters drifting to One Nation, by showing that the Coalition was not soft on protecting Australia's borders.

Brown immediately branded the Tampa incident a 'black period' in Australia's history that would severely damage Australia's international reputation. 'There has never been a situation as critical and as damaging as this to Australia's reputation,' he said. 'It has occurred in an era where the government professes globalisation but has been found to have no heart and no stomach, let alone any regard, for the spirit of international obligations to which we are a party.'

A few days later, the Greens launched their revamped immigration policy, which stated that the Greens are opposed to the detention of asylum seekers, favouring Australia's old system of integrating asylum seekers into the community and sending proven cheats home.

Despite being accused of political opportunism, Bob Brown insisted the launch was necessary because the events of the past week around the *Tampa* incident had 'undermined Australia's international reputation'. 'Australia's standing as a global citizen is under question as is Australia's commitment to international conventions on human rights,' he said.

In a speech delivered to the National Press Club on 25 September 2001 entitled 'The Greens: a Rock of Security in the Senate', Brown spelt out the party's position as both Beazley and Howard prepared to introduce the controversial mandatory detention system for refugees:

Today, Mr Howard's and Mr Beazley's parties are working to ram through seven bills cutting not only the rights of asylum seekers, but those Australians wishing to help them. The bills overrule access to the courts, bring in mandatory sentencing for the first time in federal law, and retrospectively, cover any illegal act Mr Ruddock or his officers may have committed during the *Tampa* fiasco, these are more steps towards the Australia of Pauline Hanson. That Mr Howard has moved her way may not surprise some. That Mr Beazley has gone with him is astonishing. On top of the global events hitting the economy, the mishandling of the *Tampa* affair will cost Australians dearly . . .

For the Greens, who had been the only party consistently speaking out over the government's distortions of the *Tampa* incident and generally hardline immigration policy, it was a moment of galvanising considerable and longstanding support from the voting public. Many voters noticed the fact that Bob Brown had been the only parliamentary voice speaking out against the *Tampa* machinations, *as they happened.*

No-one in the ALP was willing to speak out against it until Beazley (reluctantly) set the lead days later. Even the Democrats (who took up the issue later with zeal) were hanging back on the day the events unfolded.

But Bob Brown immediately branded the day the federal government attempted to turn the *Tampa* around and sent it back to Indonesia a 'black period' in Australia's history that would severely damage Australia's international reputation. Many mainstream voters agreed with him, and new Greens support came flooding in.

'Everyone was scared on the day, even the Democrats,' recalls Oquist. 'Then Bob really pursued it throughout that election.'

In the lead-up to the November 2001 federal election, the national press was sounding dire warnings for the Greens. 'Lobbyists across the country are putting a brave face on the polls, which put Brown's primary vote somewhere between 9.5 and 11.5 per cent. A Senate defeat for Brown could be as crushing for the budding green movement as Pauline Hanson's loss was for One Nation,' warned the *Australian*.

But the Greens' stance on asylum seekers resonated with voters.

After the 2001 election, the Greens had doubled their national vote to over 4 per cent, and Bob Brown's personal vote in Tasmania had jumped from 9 per cent to 14 per cent. This strong national vote meant that for the first time the Greens were eligible for federal funding of $1.75 for each vote received, bringing well over $1 million into the party's coffers.

Into Bob's second term of office, support for the Greens was surging among young people, estimated by an *Age* poll in 2002 to be at 25 per cent nationally. Former 'non-aligned left' student activist and East Timor women's advocate Kerry Nettle joined Bob in the Senate, adding to the party's media status and appeal to young people.

'Why is it that we have the best economic circumstances in history with the highest suicide rate? If we are going to turn that around, then not gross domestic product but gross domestic happiness should be the goal of parliament,' said Brown in the *Australian*.

By 2002 Greens were picking up considerable support in local inner city seats around Melbourne. They picked up four out of nine seats in the Yarra City Council, which takes in the Melbourne inner suburbs of Richmond and Fitzroy, traditionally Labor strongholds. The successful Greens candidates, including Greg Barber who was later to become Australia's first Greens mayor, said the party had been successful by door-knocking the entire area and sidestepping the media, in the old-school Labor fashion.

By the time George W. Bush announced his war plans for Iraq in February 2003, Bob Brown was again in the hot seat as the country's most trusted and articulate voice against Australia's involvement in the war. Issues of military involvement have always been difficult for the Greens, as they attract many old-school pacifists among party ranks. When the German Greens decided to support the sending of troops to Afghanistan in 2002, the party lost significant grassroots support in Germany. Many commentators pointed to promises the German Greens had made never to support sending German troops into a combat situation—they were seen by many as having sold out on this core promise and principle.

However, when the Australian Greens was the first political party to support the deployment of Australian troops in East Timor, this was not a divisive issue for the party. It was generally accepted as the right thing to do. Nonetheless, Ben Oquist says that the issue of where the party stands in regard to pacifism is something that will have to be resolved as it looks more seriously at assuming real political power.

'I do think the lesson for the Australian Greens to deal with pacifism has been learnt,' he says. 'Yes, the German Greens supported sending troops to Afghanistan, but they were also the reason Europe didn't support the war with Iraq. People think it was France, etc. But . . . the strongest position was taken by the German government. The reason for that was the Greens. Why could France take such a strong position? Because it wasn't isolated from Germany. I think that's why Europe wouldn't support the war on Iraq.'

Bob Brown was not mincing his words in opposing John Howard's support for sending Australian troops to Iraq as the lead-up to the war intensified. By 18 March, just days before Howard committed Australian troops, Brown issued this statement:

This is an intelligent, strong, proud nation—and the Prime Minister, at the behest of another President, is acting as if that didn't count, as if that isn't so—and he's wrong. He's waiting on one phone call to tell Australians what they already know. The Prime Minister's decision to send Australian troops into a Bush-led attack on Baghdad is undemocratic, illegal, unwarranted and puts the spilling of Australian blood squarely on his shoulders.

As early as September 2002, as the US administration was making it clear to the world that an attack on Iraq was imminent, the Australian Greens emerged as the most outspoken political party in the country against the war. On 12 September 2002—just a year after the September 11 attacks, George W. Bush addressed the United Nations, giving his clearest indication that the US would not stand by and allow Saddam Hussein to maintain power in Iraq.

'By breaking every pledge—by his deceptions, and by his cruelties—Saddam Hussein has made the case against himself,' said President George W. Bush to the UN Security Council, paving the way for the US to topple the Iraqi regime by force. The Greens joined a coalition—which included the ACTU, Catholic Commission for Justice and Peace, Australian Civil Liberties Union and a range of environmental, social justice and peace organisations—in opposing any attack on Iraq.

By the middle of January 2003, Prime Minister Howard had committed 2000 Australian troops to join what Bush called a 'coalition of the willing' to stand by for war in the Gulf. Although the Prime Minister insisted right up until the war started that the Australian troops were stationed alongside British and US military personnel in an effort to assist in the diplomatic solution to the crisis, Howard's troop deployment was widely recognised as a pre-emption to Australian involvement in a US-led war. This was despite opinion polls published at the time putting three-quarters of the Australian population against the Prime Minister's position and opposed to a US-led war without UN backing.

'The Prime Minister, and his government are far more concerned with troops being at the massacre on time than hearing the concerns of the Australian people,' said New South Wales Greens Senator Kerry Nettle. 'The rhetoric from the US administration has all but announced the declaration of war, and their fawning allies, Australia and the UK, are now in full preparation for their bit parts in this needless slaughter.' She went on:

> These troop deployments are the latest in a line of indicators that this government intends to take Australians to war irrespective of the outcomes at the UN Security Council. The Minister's contention that these troop movements are part of the Government's commitment to a 'diplomatic solution' is laughably misleading. The Government has failed to pursue a serious diplomatic peace process, instead slavishly following the US administration's aggressively reckless military policy. It's simply not the job of the Australian Defence Force to fight US oil wars.

Following on from the Greens' high political profile throughout the *Tampa* incident, the impending war on Iraq again placed the party at centre stage of the massive Australian anti-war movement—precipitating perhaps the largest anti-war protests ever seen in Australia, certainly the largest prior to a war breaking out. All around the country, Greens addressed anti-war rallies—Kerry Nettle addressed school students in Canberra and Bob Brown in particular, who addressed the biggest rallies in Melbourne and Sydney, became the pre-eminent spokespeople for the left in Australia throughout the war on Iraq.

The Global Greens issued a statement in early February denouncing the war:

> The Global Greens continue to condemn the regime of Saddam Hussein, in particular its blatant violation of human

rights and the rights of minorities such as the Kurdish people . . .

The preparedness of the United States, Britain and supporting governments to act unilaterally against Iraq, despite the fact that the United Nations weapons inspectors have been accepted by the Iraq government and are still at work, despite the fact that Iraq has not attacked any country and is not a threat to world and regional peace, is worrying. The control over oil production and distribution in the area should not be the cause of suffering for millions of innocent civilians.

The Global Greens' statement further supported the French–German peace plan for Iraq, tabled at the UN in mid-February, which was quickly dismissed by the US and Britain. While welcoming the announcement of France, Germany and Belgium that they would veto a second UN resolution pushing ahead with military action before the UN weapons inspectors had completed their task, the statement said, 'A war against Iraq will destabilise the whole Middle East region and is contrary to the spirit of the United Nations Charter and the Geneva Convention'.

At the rallies that erupted all over Australia in late February, Brown spoke of this war not being Australia's war at all—but being the war of John Howard, Tony Blair and George Bush. He spoke of the need to allow the UN weapons inspectors to carry out their work in the Gulf. He spoke of the common humanity and people power of those marching 'for a better way'. The atmosphere at the rally in Melbourne was electric. Up to a quarter of a million people crammed Melbourne's CBD and Federation Square—and because of the time zone, Melbourne became the first city in the world to stage an anti-war rally on such a massive scale, before the wave of protest spread globally over the weekend.

It was the high point of what turned out to be a huge year for Bob Brown and the Greens in Australia. But it would only be a few months down the track that Brown would take up the opportunity to spell out his feeling about Bush in a more direct forum.

❧ ❧ ❧

There was Bob Brown, at the age of 58, heckling the world's most powerful man, George W. Bush, in the Australian Parliament on 22 October 2003. It was a significant turning point for Brown and the Greens, dramatically dividing national public opinion and perhaps more than ever giving Brown a direct hearing in the international media.

Inside the Greens' Canberra office that overcast Wednesday, the tension and nervous energy preceding President Bush's speech was overwhelming. Bob Brown and his staffers had talked about the possibility of using the opportunity to make a point, but it was agreed that any interjection would be a spontaneous, rather than contrived, response to the content of the US President's speech.

Bob and his personal assistant Ben Oquist had talked it over and decided that the issue to raise with the President, if any issue was to be raised, should be that of the Australians detained in Guantanamo Bay in Cuba. There were a million other gripes Brown could have put to Bush—the Kyoto Protocol, the war on Iraq, the Australia/US free-trade negotiations—but here was something that specifically pertained to Australia, that related to a breakdown of democratic judicial process, and an issue which Bush himself had some direct control over.

In essence, all Brown was doing was exercising his right as a parliamentarian to speak in the house to which he was elected. But it was the way he did it that got up the nose of many commentators: having the gall to interrupt the US President mid-flight.

However, over the following days the Letters pages of the nation's newspapers told a different story—Brown was described as a 'true patriot' and lionised as the only member of the Australian Parliament willing to speak up in challenge to the US President.

There were others harbouring serious misgivings about Australia–US relations, in the ALP in particular (including Mark Latham, who had some weeks earlier described John Howard as an 'arse-licker' for his acquiescence to the US President) but the voices of dissent within the ALP were quietened on this day.

Oquist sat in the Greens' Canberra office watching Bush's speech live on the Parliament House monitors. The first half of the speech was full of nothing one could argue with—just the stock-standard declaration about democracy and patriotism in a world gripped by the War on Terror. But when Bush started talking about respecting the democracy and human rights of other countries, Oquist knew Bob wouldn't be able to remain silent. 'I said to my colleague, "Here we go, Bob won't be able to resist now. Watch now, watch now . . .".'

Brown stood in the parliament and heckled the President. 'Release the Australian prisoners from Guantanamo Bay.' Immediately, the efforts of some ALP members at protest—the wearing of peace badges, the refusal to applaud the President—seemed weak and wimpish. Bob Brown was the only one with the guts to really get the President's attention.

'In all the time I've been working with Bob, nothing has felt as significant as that. Nothing was as big, nothing was as nerve-racking, nothing had the same response after it,' says Oquist.

Before exiting the parliament, after earlier ignoring the orders of the speaker Neil Andrew to leave, Brown managed to give George W. Bush a firm two-handed handshake, look him squarely in the eye, and say: 'Mr Bush, this is Australia. Respect our nation. Return our Australian citizens from Guantanamo Bay. If you respect the world's laws the world will respect you.'

Within fifteen seconds of Brown making his point to Bush, the phones in the Greens office went crazy. 'Mostly local media to start with,' says Oquist, 'then international media, then members of the public.' On top of the barrage of phone calls, over the next week the Greens office received more than 5000 emails pertaining to the incident, 400 arriving within the first hour. It was the same in Greens state offices all over the country.

Herald Sun writer Andrew Bolt, who by this time had become one of the most outspoken critics of Brown (as well as being the leading columnist in the country's leading tabloid) immediately responded. He wrote a piece, accompanied by a massive picture of Brown, headed, 'Dangerous Fanatic' the following Monday.

Bolt wrote that Brown's heckling of Bush 'reminds me that Greens in the past were willing recruits to the Nazis, and explains why they today form the parliamentary party most likely to inspire violence'. He went on to remind readers that, 'in pre-war Germany, nature-worshipping was as strong as it is now. Forests were sacred, and even the Nazis encouraged organic farming. Hitler was a vegetarian who banned vivisection and created the first national parks, denouncing "people [who] attempt to rebel against the iron logic of nature". '

Bolt, in his unique way, was sensing the threat that the Greens were posing. Here was a party on 8 per cent of the national vote and rising, with an election year imminent. Bolt knew that no other party could claim to attract the kind of media interest and respect for an individual politician that the Greens command under Bob Brown. He was injecting fear of the rise of the Greens into his readership, as radio shock jocks had been doing since the day of Brown's challenge to Bush in the parliament.

Brown had demonstrated again in the federal parliament his ability to discern opportune political moments. In fact, what he did was a political masterstroke—demonstrating to the Australian public precisely which party is willing to give voice to the dissent that is brewing just below the surface of mainstream public opinion.

Not even John Howard managed to get the kind of international press coverage, beamed around the world via CNN, that Bob Brown achieved in parliament that week. CNN reported, under the headline 'Bush Hecklers Ordered Out' that President Bush was criticised both 'inside the Australian parliament and out'. Bob Brown's interjection became the focus of CNN's coverage of Bush's visit, with US reporters interviewing Brown exclusively after the event.

What other small-party politician in Australia (or large-party politician for that matter) gets to communicate so directly to the world?

'I didn't shout anything,' Brown told CNN, 'I spoke very loudly so that President Bush got the message about the two Australians who are illegally held at Guantanamo Bay after President Bush repatriated the four Americans from that hellhole.'

It was a simple message, but it's hard to think of another occasion when George W. Bush had been so directly and concisely challenged—anywhere.

Brown's interjection also gave President Bush the opportunity to display a rare streak of irony and good-humouredness when he replied after Kerry Nettle and Bob Brown's further interjections over the forthcoming free trade agreement between the US and Australia: 'I love free speech'. It made a very effective sound bite, as did Bob's immediate reply: 'So do we . . .'

The parliamentary stoush ultimately served both Bush and Brown extremely well politically. A month later, America announced that the Australians being held at Guantanamo Bay would now receive legal representation. Ben Oquist believes that Brown's interjection had a direct impact.

'In retrospect it doesn't seem so remarkable that Bob did what he did,' says Oquist. 'But it's like going to a wedding, listening to the . . . groom's speech, and deciding to interject on it. Now magnify that by a million per cent, and you get a sense of the nervous energy. It just felt like an impossible thing to do. The whole system and apparatus is designed to crush you deep down. The deep sense that you just can't do something. It's not actually a physical thing that's restraining you, but it's still there. And it felt like an amazing thing to break out of when Bob did that. It felt such a relief when he'd done it.'

The confrontation with Bush came six years and one month into Bob Brown's time in the national Senate. The very next day, the Greens were banned from attending Chinese President Hu's speech in parliament; the Australian Government was clearly keen to avoid any embarrassing repeat performance of the previous day. 'We did feel very angry about being banned from Hu's address,' he says. 'Everybody in Parliament House was complicit in that. I felt angrier than Bob did over that one—he understands that sometimes they beat you. He understands that they've got the power in the end. No matter how much right you've got on your side, this was an example that you can still be done over, that *they* still have the power.'

'Bob does have that stillness about him sometimes, not to get upset about those things. Otherwise you'd end up clawing at walls,' says Oquist.

It is consistent with the Greens' view of themselves as a global party, and Brown as an international politician, that the party would greet international visitors such as Hu and Bush with articulate and non-violent dissent.

In a speech tilted 'Factoring in Our Grandchildren', delivered to the Senate just a few days before the Bush visit, Brown had begun to articulate a new confidence and optimism around the Greens ascendancy, and the redundancy of the world's major traditional political players.

'US President George Bush, the world's most powerful man, leads the world's most global heating nation,' said Brown:

Mr. Bush should ratify the Kyoto Protocol and plan to cut greenhouse gas emissions by 60% by 2050, minimum. His choice is between his oil companies and our grandchildren. So far, he has put the grandchildren second . . .

President Hu leads the 1.3 billion people of China, the world's most populous country. It also has this finite world's most accelerating rate of consumption . . . Will President Hu announce a socially astute leapfrog of the West's car-jammed cities to mass transit systems powered by the sun, plus the world's best bikeways and pedestrian paths and planning to coordinate people's houses, workplaces and civic amenities to minimise transport needs? No, he's leap-frogging from Maoist communism to American capitalism with all market fundamentalism's problems in his booked-through baggage.

Brown concluded his speech noting that:

Presidents Bush and Hu, like Prime Minister Howard, will not deliver! Their track records show they are largely incapable of factoring future global security into their thinking except in military terms. We are not waiting for them. We aim to replace them in this century of ecotechnology and democratic global governance, with a new breed of astutely Green Presidents and Prime Ministers who will give our grandchildren the priority they deserve, not the problems we have left unsolved.

This was a new language for Brown and the Greens. At the risk of sounding like a zealot, he was introducing an important idea into the consciousness of Australian politics, something that he had hinted at all along but was now unpacking into the mainstream political dialogue. Following in the footsteps of German Greens, the Australian Greens' aspirations were not just as a fringe opposition party, or an ALP preference machine.

Brown was making it patently clear that the party is aiming to challenge mainstream local, national and international political power structures to the core. That meant seeking real political power and taking it.

For the Australian Greens at the end of 2003 this still had the ring of a distant pipe dream—even though 'Bob Brown for PM' T-shirts were starting to appear in Melbourne and Sydney coffee shops. Even though Bob Brown had been voted Australia's most 'culturally influential' person for 2003 by the *Australian Financial Review Magazine*.

For the most part, the Australian national media are not willing to report, much less champion, Brown's optimistic, aspirational politics for the Greens. Not yet, anyway.

Oquist says Brown frequently talks with that kind of confidence at Greens events and functions, and that it is necessary to articulate such ideas if they are ever to be realised. 'With Bush and Hu in town that week, Bob knew then was the time to talk big-picture,' says Oquist. 'He knows that unless you're ambitious like that, you will never get there. A lot of people think it's impossible and therefore you can't talk about it—a lot of things seem impossible before they happen.'

'Sanctimonious prick' was Democrat leader Andrew Bartlett's immediate response to Brown's interjection of Bush. The Democrats' bitter and dismissive response is not surprising; the Greens were by this stage regularly out-polling them nationally, and Brown himself garnering media coverage above and beyond that of most other politicians in the country. Although no-one in the Democrats was coming out and saying it, there may have been some within the party starting to regret that they hadn't taken the opportunity to join the Greens when that carrot was waved in the early 1980s.

By the time Natasha Stott Despoja replaced Meg Lees as leader, support for the Democrats had dropped to its lowest ever. In August 2002, the *Australian* news poll put nationwide support of the Democrats at 3 per cent, while support for the Greens nationally had topped 6 per cent. New leader Andrew

Bartlett did not help the profile of the party when in December 2003 he temporarily stood down as party leader following a drunken incident in the Senate Chamber. In contrast to the fortunes of the Democrats, the Greens have raced ahead of the Democrats in every poll in the country.

❦ ❦ ❦

Nationally speaking, in early 2004 the Greens held a record seventeen MPs in Australia's federal and state parliaments (one in the House of Representatives and two in the Senate, four in Tasmania, three in the New South Wales' upper house, five in Western Australia's upper house, one in South Australia and one in the ACT Assembly). Add to this over 50 Greens elected to local government around Australia, and the fact that in Victoria, the party won almost 16 per cent of the primary vote in the federal seat of Melbourne at the last federal election. Australia's first Green mayor, Greg Barber, was elected to head Yarra City Council, an inner Melbourne constituency.

It is a remarkable ascendancy for a party that only began to penetrate the national parliament in 1996—a mere blip in political terms. Near the completion of Brown's second term in the Senate in early 2004, it was clear that he was coming into his heyday as a federal politician. Brown was a constant fixture in the media, while only a couple of years before the party struggled to get the media to turn up to any party press conferences.

Ben Oquist is today considered one of the key architects of the Greens' rising media profile. He has worked with Bob since he entered the federal parliament in 1996, and only left the position in January 2004 to work with the European Greens.

Oquist says that over the past few years, the pressures and demands on the party have increased extraordinarily, although even when they started out in the mid-1990s he and his colleagues had high expectations for the party.

'Yes, I did expect the Greens to get to this level,' he says. 'When we started we had such high hopes. But after the struggle of the '96 and '98 campaigns, I was a bit knocked down; my confidence was slightly shaken. I remember being there in the tally room in 2001, thinking how amazing it was that this had finally happened, that we'd really made it this far. But every year I never imagine how much more work and focus and demands will be on us.'

Brown says that George W. Bush is shifting the global political paradigm, sharpening the need for the Greens to gather momentum and strength in the next decade.

'It's very frightening at the moment that Bush, in particular, is going through things like this new Patriot Act. The whole business of a society being changed in a way that completely undermines the notion of a global democracy, of one person, one vote, one value. That's why the Greens have got to keep advancing democracy. It's interesting that the extreme right—like Bush and Howard—keep talking about democracy, but it's the Greens who keep pursuing and innovating on democracy. When it gets down to it, the established governments are most interested in using the democratic system to keep themselves in power.'

Brown fully expects the party to come into their prime after he retires from the national parliament. 'If I didn't believe that, I wouldn't still be doing this,' he says.

'Talking locally and globally, I'm absolutely aware that the Greens have our ebbs and flows. I would like to see the Greens have a much stronger global interconnection, and a feeling that we're headed for opposition and government down the line. If that wasn't there, something would be seriously wrong, and there would be a need for another party that did see its role as bringing equity back to the planet, and environmental protection back onto the front burner.'

The long-term view of where the world is going—that's what the Greens bring to the table, says Brown.

'Confronting the idea that a trillion dollars is being spent on arms this year while a billion people are living in abject poverty. That situation has occurred under a long series of Labor and Coalition governments—the Greens cannot simply just become part of the jostling queue to keep delivering that kind of disparity.'

'I think . . . there is going to have to be a new form of governance that takes in the effects of human life on the biosphere. That's where the Greens started, and it's a job we haven't yet finished.'

❧ ❧ ❧

Bob Brown will turn 60 at the end of 2004, and says he is 'the happiest he has ever been'. His partnership with Paul Thomas is as strong as ever, and Bob is increasingly honing his skills as a conviction politician and insistent voice of dissent in the Australian parliament.

Despite the rise of the reinvigorated Labor Party under the leadership of Mark Latham, Brown is still frequently called upon to articulate opposition on issues where the two major parties are united, even in the face of considerable public resistance. On issues such as the Australia/US Free Trade Agreement, same-sex marriage recognition, Australia's involvement in Iraq, and his central concern of saving the Tasmanian forests from wood chippers—Bob Brown is still out there fighting the good fight.

He takes great comfort in the knowledge that he has played a significant role in the early evolution of the Australian Greens, but he takes equal delight in knowing that the party is now strong enough to survive post-Bob Brown.

Greens national campaign coordinator Andrew Burke admits that Bob is the party's 'greatest asset', but remains confident of the party's future. 'People believe that Bob believes what he says, and given how cynical people are about politicians that's quite remarkable,' says Burke. 'He's a recognised face with credibility; he's associated with very strong values. I think his political skills are commonly underrated, and dismissed as populism or grandstanding.

'But history will see him as one of the outstanding political talents of his generation.'

Much to the chagrin of some rank-and-file ALP members, Mark Latham announced in June 2004 that Australian environmentalist and former Midnight Oil lead singer Peter Garrett would be installed to run for the Labor Party in the safe seat of Kingsford Smith in Sydney. Bob Brown and Paul Thomas count Peter Garrett as a personal friend, having attended the former singer's 50th birthday party in 2003 by personal invitation. Bob Brown and Peter Garrett have also rafted the Franklin together, and worked side by side on many environmental campaigns over the past decades.

Having confessed to not being an environmentalist himself, Mark Latham sought to lure back the Green vote, bringing a respected celebrity with a full deck of Green credentials into the Labor Party. Brown welcomes the move, particularly if it means the ALP will adopt better environmental policy, stating, however that he fears for Garrett's welfare within the ALP party machine. 'The question is, who prevails?' said Brown on 11 June 2004.

'Does Peter change the party on the forests, or does he accede to the ALP's chainsaws-rule policy? It has to be one or the other. I am alarmed by Peter having to commit to current ALP policy.'

Either way, the appointment of Garrett signifies that the environment will continue to be a crucial issue in the Australian political landscape in the new millennium. The role of the Greens will grow accordingly. 'There's no doubt that Bob will be missed when he does go, but the core values of the party are rock solid and will be reflected by a new leader,' says Burke. 'Although Bob is a wonderful leader, we're not dependent upon him in the way that One Nation was with Pauline Hanson. We are deeply integrated into the community and our policies are widely understood.'

Meanwhile, on a final visit to Bob's place in Liffey, sitting on the front porch on a crisp clear morning, I'm struck by how deeply Bob Brown is a rare living example of the potential for positive transformation that becomes possible for individuals and communities when ideals and action fuse.

Reflecting on the thirty years since Bob purchased the bush shack and adjoining lands, these forests that Bob himself had a direct hand in saving have, in turn, been instrumental in empowering him. For what better a source of personal rejuvenating power, what better a reminder of one's humanness within the natural world than the soothing sounds and aspect of these forested hills and valleys in Central North Tasmania.

Such as it is at Bob Brown's front porch in Liffey.

Acknowledgments and notes on sources

There are a number of people to whom I am indebted for their help in providing the information required for writing this book.

I should firstly thank Gregg Borchmann, whose excellent and exhaustive interview with Bob Brown helped greatly in getting this project kick-started. Gregg Borschmann, Executive Director of The Peoples Forest Foundation Ltd, recorded the interview for the 'My Country' Oral History Collection, in association with the National Library of Australia in March 1994.

Secondly, I should acknowledge Peter Thompson, whose book *Bob Brown of the Franklin River* proved an invaluable resource. Peter was also very helpful in the interviews I conducted with him.

Acknowledgment also to the extremely kind and considered Judy Henderson, whose responses helped to flesh out Bob's teenage life in particular. Bob's partner Paul Thomas was also of great help in gathering information, being interviewed, and checking the accuracy of this book.

I should also extend my thanks to the staff of the *Age* Library in Melbourne, who freely gave their time and expertise in tracking down the several hundred articles I used in piecing together Bob's political life.

Other sources I should mention include Drew Hutton in Queensland, Ben Oquist who came down to Melbourne expressly to see me at the Garden of Eden, Rodney Croome and Nick Toonen in Hobart. Finally, I wish to pass on my respect to Deni Hammill, who passed away in early 2004, and whose brave stand in supporting and transporting the Franklin campaigners continues to inspire.

The mysterious phone call to Brenda Hean (page 58) and the reference to the Gray Government's recall of government to approve the Wesley Vale legislation (page 119) have been sourced from 'I saw my Temple Ransacked' by Kevin Kiernan and 'The Masters of History' by Richard Flanagan, *The Rest of the World is Watching*, (eds) Cassandra Pybus and Richard Flanagan, Pan Macmillan Publishers, 1990.

Thank you

In completing the journey of this book I have been fortunate enough to feel supported by fellow travellers along the way.

I was warned from the outset by Bob Brown himself that he would keep an arm's length from this project, and that I would have to seek to paint an intimate portrait of a reluctant subject. That said, the kindness, generosity and eventual openness that both Bob and Paul Thomas extended to me were just superb.

Beyond that, my heartfelt thanks go to my secret weapon and the most wonderful mother imaginable, Terry Weir. Thanks a packet also to those who helped me finalise my proofs and gave me the encouragement to keep going: Barry Norman, Amos Hee (you're a shining star), Gemma Pinnell, Doctor Craig Bellamy for keeping me on my toes, and soul mates Aaron, Matt, Dean, and Franzi.

Index